Contents

List of Illustrations

Copyright holders
    [S] Suffolk Record Office Ipswich

Photographs

[Bell]	Chris & Marcia Bell	
[B]	Michael Bryant	© 2013
[C]	Bob Clark	© 2013
[F]	Rev Farrer	1920 to 1930
[G]	Charles Greenhough	© 2013
Others	Unknown photographer	

Acknowledgements

My thanks go to the following who have shared their knowledge of the village and answered my constant questions: Michael Bailey, Mary Baxter, Chris & Marcia Bell, Nora Brier, Margaret Brown, Arthur & Gillian Bryant, Michael Bryant, Gilbert Burroughes, Anne Butcher, Brian Chandler, Linda & Ray Cook, Sarah Doig, Liz Draper, Jackie Erith, John Farrow, Robert & Rhonda Foulger, Simon Gowen, Sally Green, Neil Lanham, Jim Moule, Brenda Royal, Ken Rush, John Stratford, Stanley & Helen Sharman, Jean Sheehan, Audrey Simonds, Kenny Wilby, Melanie Wildish and Jackie Worby.

Further thanks go to all the people who kindly let me view their houses and their house deeds: Lesley Abery, Jilly & Robin Brown, Glynis & Philip Brown, Bob & Roz Clark, John & Sue Clarke, Gillian Crossley-Holland, Tim Deakin, Fay & John Dunkley, Jackie Erith, Richard Fenton, Christine Hurrell, Jeff Kennedy, Christine MacLeod, Terri McDonald, Kevin McNally, Jo & Graham Meekings, Alick & Linda Miles, Louise & Duncan Moffat, Stephen Pattenden, Fred & Joyce Ratcliffe, Philippa Rixon & Jean Philpott, Gwen & Ted Smith, Iain Smith, Andy Stubbs, Dorothy & David Wittekind.

To Sue Emerson and Graham Clayton for proof reading, Tony Emerson who drew the maps, Lesley and Charles Greenhough for type setting and checking, Tim Holt-Wilson for permission to use the Redgrave Estate Papers and Pete Everall for letting me see his research on Allwood Green.

Please remember all the houses described here are private residences and are not available for viewing.

Abbreviations

BL = British Library

NRO = Norfolk Record Office

PRO = Public Record Office now National Archives, Kew

SROI = Suffolk Record Office Ipswich

SCC = Suffolk County Council

iv

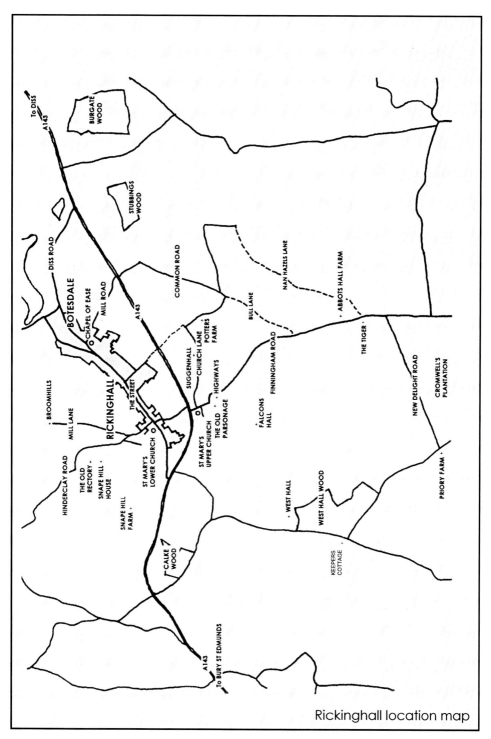

Rickinghall location map

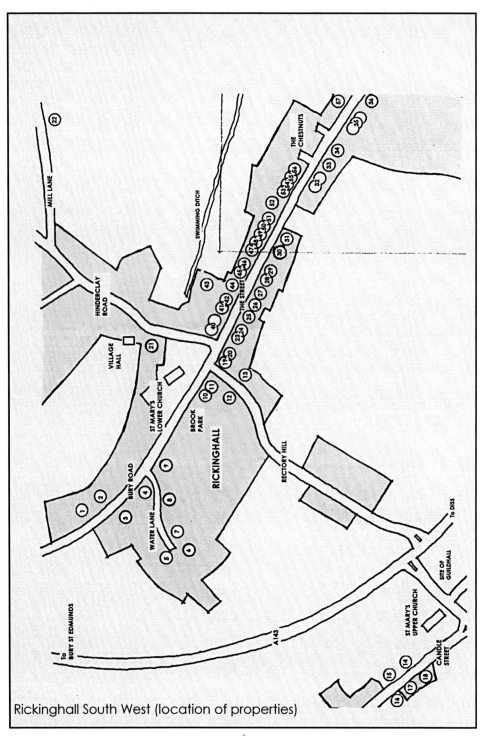

Rickinghall South West (location of properties)

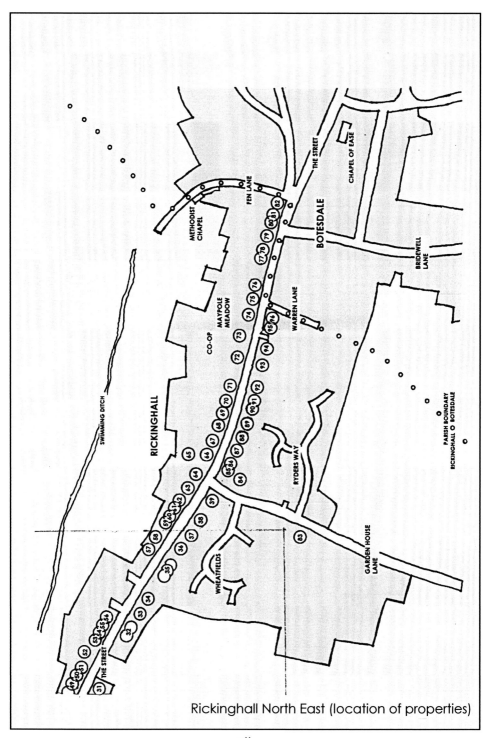

Rickinghall North East (location of properties)

Key to house names

1. Tudor Cottage
2. The Old Vicarage
3. Stanley Cottage
4. Bridge House
5. Rose Cottage and Croft Cottage
6. Riverslea
7. Crooked Cottage
8. Old Coach House
9. Brook House
10. Bell Cottage
11. Wall Cottage
12. Hanby
13. The Mount
14. Kiln Cottage
15. Cherry Tree House
16. Kiln Farm House
17. 3 & 4 Kiln Farm Cottages
18. 1 & 2 Kiln Farm Cottages
19. Breklaw
20. Rossendale Cottage
21. The Old School
22. Mill House & Mill Cottage
23. Linden House
24. Forge Cottage
25. Shemmings

26. Tiger Cottage & Forge Close
27. Lavender Cottage
28. Hall House Cottage
29. Tipplers
30. The Old Bakery
31. The White Horse
32. North View
33. Stanwell House
34. Daisy Cottage
35. Glenfield, Meadow View, Chestnut View
36. White Gate
37. Redholme
38. Old Railway Carriage
39. Walsingham Mews
40. Church Farm House and Cottage
41. The Old Post Office
42. Lamorna Cottage
43. Church Farm Barn
44. Little Patches
45. Hazel Cottage
46. Baylees
47. Old Timbers
48. Flint Cottage
49. Vine Cottage

Introduction

The aim of this guide is not to provide a history of the village itself, but to take you on a walk through Rickinghall Inferior and Superior and tell you as much of the history of each house and area as I have been able to find from research and information from the people who grew up in the village. It is hoped that this book will also act as a useful guide for those wanting to research the history of their houses or local history. It is based on the latest information available but as more comes to light some of this may change.

The villages of Rickinghall, together with the neighbouring village of Botesdale, have a number of interesting buildings including good examples of houses from the last 500 years, the oldest dating from the 15th century. In some cases these are easy to recognise, but many were extended and brick-faced in later centuries when timber-framed houses had become old fashioned and people wanted their houses to appear modern.

The name Rickinghall is a Saxon name meaning corner or nook of the people of Rica. Rickinghall is in fact two villages: Rickinghall Inferior and Rickinghall Superior. In the past Rickinghall Inferior has also been known as Lower, Nether or Parva and Rickinghall Superior has been known as Over, Upper or Magna. It is thought that the two villages were at one time one village and were divided into two in the 11th century.

Rickinghall Inferior had one manor: the manor of Westhall. It had belonged to Ulfcytel (Ulfketel), a Saxon earl, who gave the manor to the Abbot of Bury St Edmunds in about 1005. In 1544, after the dissolution, it was granted to Sir Nicholas Bacon. In the early 1700s it was sold by the Bacon family to Chief Justice Sir John Holt. In the late 18th century it passed by inheritance to the Wilson family.

Since the 13th century **Rickinghall Superior** has had various manors associated with it. The Manors were those of FitzJohns, Crowe's Hall, Facon's Hall and Talbot Hall. The last three appear to be names used at different periods for the same manor.

The Talbots of Hintlesham held the 'Manor of Rickinghall' which was often referred to as Talbotshall. In 1284 the son of William Talbot leased this manor to John and Mary Crowe who also held manors in Debenham and Crowfield. It is not certain where the manor house of Crowe's Hall was situated in Rickinghall. It could have been near the present day Suggenhall, however it is more likely to have been on the site of Facon's Hall, now called Falcon's Hall. It is thought the name Facon's Hall comes from Walter Faukon who married Joan Talbot widow of Thomas Talbot in 1305. The Talbot family held Facon's Hall until it came into the possession of the Hervy family in the 15ᵗʰ century. In 1507 the Yaxley family were in possession. They sold it to Sir Nicholas Bacon in 1599 and from then until 1896 it was held by the lords of the manor of Redgrave.

The manor of FitzJohns was, according to Copinger, held in 'ancient times' by John FitzJohn, and in 1428 by the Bishop of Chichester. (1) In the early 16ᵗʰ century it came into the possession of the Yaxley family. In 1566 it was acquired by Sir Nicholas Bacon. There does not seem to have been a manor house associated with it at any time.

In the past, villages were self-sufficient and the Rickinghalls were no exception; anything people could not grow or make themselves they could buy in the villages. The main road through the villages led to Botesdale which, from the early 1200s, had a thriving Thursday Market. It appears that there were shops and businesses all along the village street to attract the visitors passing through as well as catering to the needs of the villagers themselves. There were butchers, tanners, grocers, tailors, cobblers, carpenters, drapers, brewers, bakers, inns and taverns from the medieval period until very recently. The main occupation however was agriculture and businesses that relied on agriculture, such as milling and malting. Today Botesdale and Rickinghall between them still have several businesses and pubs and several shops.

The walk starts at the crossroads near the Lower Church and goes to each lane or road in turn and out to the outlying areas of the villages. To make it easier to follow, this guide has been divided into nine chapters.

Di Maywhort

(1) Copinger, Vol. I page 357, Vol. III page 297

St Mary The Virgin, Rickinghall Inferior from the west

St Mary's Rickinghall Inferior church is a round tower church mentioned in the Domesday survey of 1086. The tower was built in the late 11th century and was heightened by an octagonal belfry in the 14th century. The belfry contains three bells, the earliest dating from about 1350 and the others from about 1500 and from 1636. The chancel dates to the 13th century. The nave was rebuilt in the 14th century apart from the north wall which appears to be the original Norman wall with 15th century door and windows inserted. The porch was built in the 14th century with an upper chamber or parvise added in the 15th century. Unfortunately the stairs going to this have been blocked. The flint flushwork above the porch archway imitates the work of the Aldrych family firm of stone masons from North Lopham who worked in Suffolk from 1487 to 1508. Much of the church was restored in 1858/9 at the time of the Revd Maul.

Most of the stained glass is Victorian; however there are a few pieces of medieval glass in the south east window of the chancel. The glass in the east window of the south aisle was inserted to commemorate the Millennium and was made by Eric Eckersley. The bier, used to carry the coffins, is very like the one in the upper church which is dated 1763. The Roll of Honour boards commemorate the men from the village who died

in the two world wars. A Roman Samian-ware type plaque has recently been donated by The Suffolk Institute of Archaeology and History in memory of Basil Brown. It depicts Basil with the Sutton Hoo ship behind him. It was made by Gilbert Burroughes, an expert in Roman pottery, who was born in the village. (1)

Samian-ware style plaque in memory of Basil Brown

Across the road from the church on the corner of Bury Road and Rectory Hill is **Wall Cottage** which is an early 16th century building. Upstairs there are carpenters' marks on many of the timbers; there is also a shutter groove which is evidence for a medieval window. A brass plate on the principal joist in the sitting room has the inscription 'Built 1525 Restored 1963'; however no evidence has been found for the precise date of 1525. It appears that the cottage was originally divided into two and usually occupied by tenants. It was possibly a shop from at least the 18th century. Photographs from the early 20th century show a shop on the premises and two front doors. It appears that the first Post Office in Rickinghall opened here in 1890. Henry Hayward was the first sub-postmaster.

Brook House is an early 18th century building which was re-fronted in about 1830 and extended in the mid 19th century. The Amys family owned the house in the 18th and early 19th centuries. The Tuck family inherited it from the Amys (Mrs Tuck was a Miss Amys). Colonel Hasted lived here from 1900 until 1916. His grandson, Frederick Thackeray, whose name is on the War Memorial, was killed in 1915. Colonel Hasted died soon afterwards. The Tuck family lived here until the 1950s. Colonel Tuck commanded the local Home Guard unit during the Second World War. **Brook Park** was named in the 1990s when the houses were built there.

A milestone is still in place standing by the churchyard hedge. According to the listing it is dated to the late 18th or early 19th century and is inscribed '9m(iles) To Scole, 14m To Bury, 96m To London, 27m To Norwich'. Unfortunately the writing on it is now illegible.

Water Lane leads off to the left between Brook House and Bridge House. It becomes a footpath which crosses the bypass and ends at Candle

Street. A lane called Bush Lane led off to the right just after The Cottage, it ran parallel with Briar Lane, passed north of West Hall Farm and ended at West Street. It was closed at the time of the Enclosure Awards. There was also a Bush Meadow nearby.

The **Old Coach House** as the name implies was the coach house to Brook House. It was probably built in the early 19th century when Brook House was enlarged.

The Whistlecraft family lived in Water Lane in one side of a divided house which has now been demolished. The house built on the site is called **Hunters Lodge**. Henry and John Whistlecraft, who were brothers, died in the First World War. John had returned from Canada to fight but served under the name of James Smith. The family were well known poachers in the 19th and early 20th century.

The Pightle is a prefabricated bungalow that was built in the early 1960s and was later brick clad.

Crooked Cottage is a thatched timber-framed two bay building with a crown post dating from the late 15th century, about 1480. It is a former open hall house and still has soot on the rafters in the roof. In these medieval hall houses the hall was open to the roof, a hearth was situated in the middle of the floor to warm the room and on which the cooking was done. There was no chimney so the smoke would go straight to the roof blackening the rafters. In the late 16th century it became fashionable (and more practical) to add a chimney stack and fireplace at one end of the hall so the central hearth became redundant. In Crooked Cottage the chimney stack and floor were added in the 17th century and later some areas were faced with brick. For many years it was divided into two dwellings.

Crown post in Crooked Cottage

Riverslea is a timber-framed cottage probably dating from the 18th century but it could be earlier. In 1819 it was owned by Patrick Thomas Senior. He still owned it in 1839 when it was

3

occupied by James King, a butcher. The Bailey family owned it from the early 20th century, Frederick Bailey, chairman of the parish council for many years, was born here in 1909.

The Cottage was a thatched cottage which was partly demolished and rebuilt with a tiled roof in the 1980s.

On the right behind The Cottage is a thatched building now divided into two and called **Croft Cottage** and **Rose Cottage.** It stood beside Bush Lane. According to the listings it is an early 16th century building. A blocked diamond mullion window in an inside wall indicates where the original building ended. An extension was added perhaps 50 to 100 years after the original build. This is probably the cottage referred to in the Hanby deeds of 1686 when Francis Symonds, a linen weaver, died and left the cottage to his wife and mother-in-law. John Steggles appears to have acquired it in 1749 along with other properties. The deeds refer to a shop being part of the cottage at this time. In 1815 Elizabeth Hixxer transferred the property to another John Steggles, a bricklayer. When he died in 1826 a third John Steggles acquired it. He rented it out to under tenants. He also borrowed money from Edward and Alfred Colson using it as collateral. In 1892 Mary Colson, widow of Alfred, sold it to James Pearce who in turn sold it in 1935 to Annie Garnham. It appears that by this time it was divided into two dwellings. The Garnham family owned Croft Cottage until 1982 when Jack Garnham died and the present owner bought it.

Rose Cottage was occupied by the Powell family from the early 1950s. After his wife's death, Sandy Powell was accepted as a Chelsea Pensioner. One year he came back for a Remembrance parade and wore his distinctive red uniform to take the salute.

Water Lane has always had a stream (usually called The River), which originates in the fields beyond Falcon's Hall and runs down beside the lane. It crosses the lane near Riverslea where there is now a bridge but where there used to be a ford. The stream called the Swimming Ditch joins it half way down the lane. This was a lovely clear little river which never ran dry. It had water cress and sticklebacks in it with water voles living on the banks. However when the houses were put onto mains water the whole river bed was dug up to lay the pipes and the river has never been the same since, often drying up completely.

At the junction of Water Lane and Bury Road, **Bridge House** is a late 16th century house that was altered and extended in the 19th and 20th centuries. It has a jetty on the south side indicating that this was once the

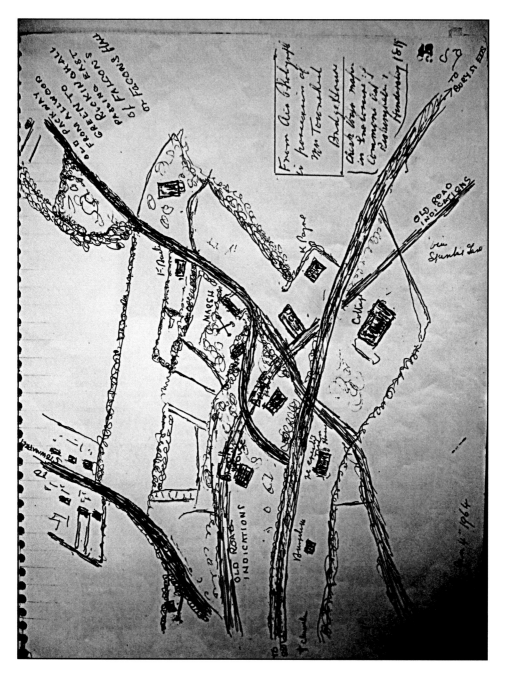

Basil Brown's sketch map of the possible route of old roads in Rickinghall

front and that this is the side that used to face the original road.

It seems that the Bury Road used to go down what is now the drive of Stanley Cottage, to what used to be the front (and is now the back) of Bridge House, across Water Lane and continue approximately where Brook House is today,

Bridge House

nearly forming two sides of a triangle. It appears like this on the Enclosure Map of 1819 but on the 1839 Tithe Map the road is in its present position. It is possible that when Brook House was extended in the 1830s it was decided to alter the road, making it straighter and taking it away from the house.

Stanley Cottage is a thatched early 16th century timber-framed open hall house, the stack and floor of which were inserted in the late 16th century.

Tudor House is probably a 16th century house. It was moved from Stowmarket in 1958. Timber-framed houses were often moved in the medieval period. They were originally built in the carpenter's yard and each timber throughout the house would be numbered so they could be easily assembled on the chosen site. It was therefore easy to take down and reassemble them. They were in fact the first type of 'prefabricated' houses.

The Old Vicarage, until recently called The Cottage, is thought to date from the 16th century, but very little of this original house remains. The Amys family who owned much land in Rickinghall lived here in the 18th and 19th centuries. They probably bought it from the Freeman family who in turn had acquired it from the Beale family. Mr & Mrs Flowerdew bought the house in 1931 and lived here from 1936. During 1944 the pilots of planes towing gliders practising for the D Day landings would look for the distinctive diamond pattern on the roof before dropping their tow ropes. The ropes could later be retrieved from a field opposite Calke Wood. (2) In the 1930s one of the Flowerdew children developed tuberculosis and used to spend his days in the study situated in the garden. He went to

Rickinghall Silver Band and The Foresters in front of
The Cottage (before 1914)

Switzerland for treatment but had to return in the late 1930s. His nurse, a Swiss national, returned with him and he later married her to prevent her being interned as an alien. (3) In the 1950s Mrs Flowerdew held choir practice at her home every week and held parties for the village children at Christmas.

According to Basil Brown the following names are scratched on the cellar window: Mary Amys July 1776, Eleanora Jacot March 12th 1777, John Amys 1809, however these are not there now. Perhaps they are on some other window in some other house? It would be interesting to find where these are.

Low Meadow is a small meadow that was given to the villages of Rickinghall by the Barker family in 1997. It is now managed by Barwoods (Botesdale and Rickinghall Community Woodlands Group) which is creating a wildflower meadow there. It used to have a large pond and several smaller ones along the stream.

Briar Lodge is a flint cottage built between 1819 and 1839 as a lodge to Snape Hill House. A drive used to go from Briar Lodge to Snape Hill House. Briar Lane leads across the bypass from opposite the house.

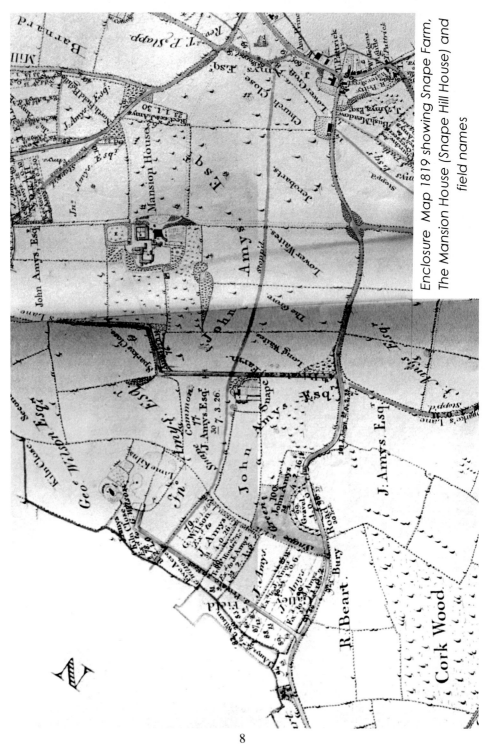

Enclosure Map 1819 showing Snape Farm, The Mansion House (Snape Hill House) and field names

Snape Farm was once the farm attached to Snape Hill House. The listings say it is an early 17th century three bay lobby entry timber-framed house, possibly with earlier origins, which was brick fronted in the 19th century. In 1437 John Gelder held a messuage or dwelling house with outbuildings very close to the present site. By the 1608 extent it appears to have been in the occupation of John Hyll but this is not clear; he certainly held most of the land surrounding Snape Farm. From the 18th century it was the farm associated with Snape Hill House. By 1774 it had come into the possession of John Amys who probably bought it from John Freeman. The Amys family owned it until the early 1840s when they sold Snape House and Snape Farm House to Thomas Norton who in turn sold them to George Holt Wilson in 1909. The Miles family moved here as tenant farmers at this time. They bought the farm from the Holt-Wilson family in 1972 and members of the family still live here.

The **Lime Kilns** and **Kiln Close** were situated to the north west of Snape Farm. In 1437 John Gelder held a field called Calklond so it appears chalk was being extracted even then. There are several land indentures dating from 1665 to 1722 when the Brown family leased the kiln and Kiln Close. (4) In 1819 the Amys family owned them, however by 1839 there appear to be two kilns, one owned by John Amys and the other by the Redgrave Estate, the latter was being worked by Samuel Bond. In the 1901 census Charles Roberts a 'whiteing maker' lived and worked at the Lime Kiln. It is not clear when the kilns stopped working. Today there is a pit from where the chalk was extracted, which is used as a shooting range. Until the mid 20th century this pit was home to the famous snails said to have been brought to the area by the Romans but after trees were dug out and the pit disturbed in the 1970s, sadly they have disappeared.

Snape Green is first mentioned in a court roll for 1273 when a William Flobar gave the lord of the manor four shillings for the right to graze four score (80) sheep there and at a place called South Wood. In 1361 Adam, son of Peter, was fined for grazing animals on Snape Green without licence. (5) Snape comes from the word 'snaep' meaning a parcel of land. (6)

Many fields around Snape Farm still have their medieval names or names very similar to the medieval ones, which is very unusual. For instance Thweytclose is now Long and Lower Waites. Sparkes Close is still Sparkes field and Foxburrows is still called by that name.

The private lane that runs north near the present lay-by on the main road leads to the old lime kiln and to the area once called **Gallows Hill or**

Meadow. There are several references to a gallows hill in this area. The first that has been found so far is in the 1437 extent when it appears to have been where it is today to the east of Snape Farm near the Lime Kilns and on the boundary between Rickinghall and Hinderclay villages. Gallows were often erected on a boundary between two villages. No evidence of felons being hanged here has yet been found.

Basil Brown thought that the original road to Bury ran north of the road that has itself been replaced by the bypass. Apparently the hill where the gallows had been situated was so steep that the horse-drawn coaches had difficulty ascending so the road was made to the south. He thought the line of very old oaks that cross the field south of Snape Farm lined the original road.

The lane leading from the old road (near the present bottle bank) goes past Snape Farm turning right and then left into Sparkes Lane, a lovely green lane, which continues until it reaches the Hinderclay Road. This was formerly called Mill Lane because it led to the medieval mill called Brommelle which it is thought was situated on 'Mill Mount' to the right of the Hinderclay road.

(1) See Quatrefoil Book Number 3 (2) Letter from Jack Corcoran See Parish magazine July 2010 (3) Information from the Flowerdew family (4) SROI HA 240/2508/312-322 (5) BL Add 40063 fo:9v & 20v (6) See Millennium Miscellany. p.75

Chapter 2 Calke Wood and West Street

Walnut Tree Farmhouse lies on the corner of the main Bury Road and Calkewood Lane which is the boundary between Rickinghall Inferior and Wattisfield. It is an early to mid 17th century timber-framed house which has a three bay lobby entrance plan with a kitchen wing to form an L shape. There is a story that the cellars extend under the road to The Black Swan forming a tunnel.

Calke Wood lies along Calkewood Lane and is an ancient wood (which is a wood that has existed continuously since 1600 or before). The first reference we have to the name Calkewood is in the 1543 extent which says *'John Trapette holds by copy …. 3 acres of the wood called Calkewood at a rent of 12d p.a.'* In the 1599 extent Thomas Wright, gentleman, owned one wood called Calkwoode which had recently belonged to John Dobbes and contained 25 acres. In 1777 Richard Clerke was on the ratepayers list in the Churchwardens' account book paying £4 2s 8d in rates for Calke Wood. On the 1839 Tithe Map it was called Cork Wood and was owned by a John Wright. It was then 23 acres 1 rood and 19 perches. Today the acreage is just over 24 acres.

As no reference to Calke Wood has been found in any documents earlier than the 16th century it is possible that it was deliberately planted as a wood in the late medieval period. There are groves of hornbeam and hazel within the wood indicating they were planted for specific uses such as making hazel hurdles. The ditches found in and surrounding the wood are thought to be medieval in origin. However, according to archaeological reports, the Calke Wood area is a 'multi period site'. (1) Basil Brown did several excavations here and found evidence of occupation as early as the Neolithic period. He also found 'Beaker' sherds. The Beaker period dates from approximately 2500 - 1700 BC. Evidence of Saxon occupation has been found in a nearby field. Opposite Calke Wood in Wattisfield is Foxledge Common where, in the 1930s, Basil Brown found 11 Roman kilns, one of which can be seen in Ipswich Museum. Clay was being extracted from Calke Wood at this time and it was still being used by Watsons Pottery in Wattisfield until the 1950s. A bungalow was built on the edge of the wood in the 1970s by Stanley Mole who made his living from constructing hurdles, gates etc. from the timber.

Until the 17th century **Calkewood Lane** used to be called the Porteway. It starts at the Bury Road and becomes West Street at a junction with Briar Lane. Briar Lane was called Tydemans Lane on both the 1819 Enclosure Map and the 1839 Tithe Map. Edmund Tydeman owned land in the area in the 18th century. Briar Lane starts opposite Briar Lodge and crosses the bypass, continuing until it joins the junction of Calkewood Lane and West Street. This junction was where Sparkes Lane used to join the other three lanes forming a crossroads. This part of Sparkes Lane was closed in 1819: the north end now starts near Snape Farm and terminates at the Hinderclay Road.

In the medieval period crossroads such as this one often had a wooden or stone cross situated beside them. These crosses were where people could pray whilst working in the fields. Several people in the medieval period have surnames 'at the Cross' or 'Rode' (rode is the medieval word for cross; as in rood screen) In 1271 Isabella Cros daughter of Walter of the Rode of Rickinghall gave the lord of the manor 12d for a licence to marry and in 1335 Adam atte Rode (at the cross) had a sheep fold for 80 sheep for which he was fined 6d. (2)

Briar Cottage is the first house in Briar Lane. It was formerly divided into two cottages, and in a sales catalogue for 1867 it was in the occupation of William Martin and Widow Rose.

Jackamans Farm on the right is now in a derelict state. It was farmed by John Jackaman from the 1830s until the 1870s and was called Sandpit Cottage at that time. In 1918 it was called Sandpit House.

Swallow Falls and **No.2**, the first houses in West Street, were built in 1938 as council houses for large families. In 1960 they were condemned as needing new foundations. New foundations were dug and the houses were sold to private owners in the early 1970s.

West Street Farm has been a farm since the 19th century. In 1839 the tenant farmer was Jacob Eaves. It is now a chicken farm.

Opposite the farm next to **West Street Cottage** there used to be two thatched cottages which burnt down in August 1943. A spark from a domestic fire started the blaze.

When the water mains were being replaced along West Street in the 1990s evidence was found of occupation in the medieval period. A 15th or 16th century pottery kiln was also found. This site is not far from Foxledge Common where the Roman kilns were found which confirms that pottery was being made in this area over many centuries. (3)

Flowing through the valley to the left of West Street is the Swimming Ditch. This stream rises in Walsham-le-Willows and runs between Trickers Meadow and Trickers cottage in Walsham on the other side of Westhall Wood

Road. It continues past West Hall Wood and West Hall and runs through Duckingstool Meadow to Water Lane where it joins another stream which starts near Falcon's Hall. It crosses the Bury Road at Bridge House and flows past Rickinghall Inferior Church, crosses the Hinderclay road and runs parallel to The Street.

The large field on the left through which the stream runs is called Duckingstool Meadow, a name it has had for centuries. There is a pond next to the stream which used to be very large and was always used as the horse pond; horses were taken there to drink after work. It is possible that this is where a ducking stool was situated. In the 1437 extent and even earlier this field was called Cokestole meadow. A coke or Cuke stool is the medieval name for a ducking stool. (4) The pond was always used for swimming by children in the early 20th century and probably before then.

West Hall Farm is probably situated on the site of the medieval manor hall. The house itself is a timber-framed early 17th century building which was extended in the late 17th century and re-fronted with brick in the late 19th century. Throughout its history it appears to have been leased or rented to tenants by the lord of the manor. This was the Abbot of Bury St Edmunds from 1005 until the Dissolution of the Abbey in 1539. In 1544 Sir Nicholas Bacon purchased the manor from the Crown. The Bacon family were lords of the manor until the end of the 17th century when the Holt family purchased the manor from them. The Wilson family inherited it from them.

West Hall in 1874. Mr & Mrs Symonds in the garden

In 1464, when William Fotour was leasing the manor, an account roll details the building of a new annex for the house at a cost of 16s 11d. Two barns, a stable, various farm buildings, a sheep byre and a gatehouse were all re-thatched at this time. The thatcher and his servant were paid 8d a day for 29 days. The straw for the thatching cost 19s 8d. (5) In 1608 Roger Seaman was leasing the demesne land of the manor. John Morrys held over 65 acres in 1642 but it is not clear if this includes West Hall itself. In 1839 John Blomfield rented the farm followed by Richard Flowerdew.

In 1849 George Symonds was the tenant and in a survey of that date it says 'The House is a commodious Farm Residence and is in good order but many of the Buildings are old and require a general repair & a new cottage has been built near the Road. The Barn requires a shed to be added to enable the Tenant to keep stock in the yard and make a supply of manure for that part of the Farm. A Stable and Shed for Cattle and Implements are also wanted here, to form a convenient yard for Cattle and to enable the Tenant to keep some of his Horses at this part of the Farm – it would be of great advantage if a Cottage was built and I have no doubt but that the Tenant would be willing to pay a full percentage on the outlay.' A large barn on the site was rebuilt just after this, reusing many timbers from an earlier building. In the 1850s and 60s intensive mixed animal husbandry known as 'Victorian High Farming' was introduced in Suffolk. Cattle were kept in enclosed yards and a series of open-sided shelter sheds were built here at this time as was suggested in the survey. A horse mill is also recorded and the present drive to the farm was made. The Symonds family continued to rent the farm until 1918 when George Holt Wilson sold it to John Hall. The Hall family have owned it ever since and it is now farmed by John Hall's great-grandson David Pettitt.

Apparently postholes of a Saxon building were discovered in a field near West Hall Farm however we have no specific information about this. If this is the case it would be further evidence that this is the area where the early hall and the associated buildings were situated when Ulfcytel held the manor before he willed it to St Edmunds Abbey in the early 11th century.

Keepers Cottage is an early 19th century house. It was called Botwright's Farm for many years. In 1849 the tenant was George Botwright and the survey says 'The buildings which are convenient, require some slight repair and the house would be much improved by forming a covered way to the wash house which could then be made to answer the purpose of a back kitchen and would add much to the comfort of the Tenant'. This covered way was never made. In Kelly's Directory for 1900 Eli Morley, gamekeeper to George Wilson lived at Botwright's Farm and it appears that this is when it received the name Keepers House which was changed to Keepers Cottage in 1990.

Westhall Wood is an ancient wood. It is designated an SSSI (Site of Special Scientific Interest). A wood, which was probably this one, was mentioned in the 1086 Domesday survey as a wood for 60 pigs. In the 1437 Extent Eltonhaughe Wood was a large wood in the demesne of the Abbot. There are many references to it both before and after this and it appears that this could be Westhall Wood. The ditches running through the wood are thought to be medieval in origin. Unfortunately so far the acreage of the wood in the medieval period has not yet been discovered. In 1918 it was 82 acres and 32 perches and today it is 83 acres.

There were several other woods in the area in the medieval period among them one called Aylesmeres Wood and another called Short Hazell Wood. Today there is a field called Shorthazell which could be where the wood once stood.

West Street continues until it reaches the road to Walsham. Just past Keepers Cottage, West Hall Road leads off to the left. **Priory Farm** is situated on the junction of this road and New Delight Road. It is a late 16th century timber-framed thatched house. 'GB 1579' and 'TMY 1579' are carved on the storey posts, which suggests that this is when it was built. However no trace of anyone with the initials GB or a TMY have so far been discovered. In 1839 it was owned by Thomas Martin. Nathaniel Martin was still farming there in 1844. In a sales catalogue for 1923, when the house was being sold on the death of William Barker, it is described as being timber-framed with four bedrooms and an apple room. Mr Elmer bought the house at this time and in the 1940s it was inherited by Mr Farrow, the grandfather of the present owner.

(1) SCC sites and Monuments Record RKN 011 (2) BL Add 40063 fo: 9 & fo: 15 (3) SCC sites and monuments records RKN 030, 031,032 (4) SROI HA 240 2508/673 (1358) (5) SROI HD 116 3/21/1.3

Chapter 3 Rectory Hill, Candle Street, Finningham Road, Allwood Green

Rectory Hill was previously called Stowe Road. On the right is **Hanby**. The deeds for this cottage date from 1686 when Francis Symonds died and his will is recorded. In 1759 John Steggles was the copyhold tenant. In the 1950s, when flocks of sheep were brought through the village and up Rectory Hill to Kiln Farm to be sheared, the lady who used to live at Hanby would run out in her dressing gown and slippers and chase the sheep away from her garden with a large stick.

The Mount was apparently once the Rickinghall Police Station before it was moved to Astley House in 1898. In the 1950s the cellars still had chains with handcuffs attached to the walls!

The houses on both sides at the top of the hill were built as council houses in the late 1930s. Sand was dug from a nearby field to use in their construction. Today the houses are mostly privately owned.

Field walking carried out in the mid 1990s by the Suffolk Archaeological Unit before the bypass was built revealed a number of worked flints where the road crosses Rectory Hill near the church. About 50 metres to the left archaeologists found large quantities of medieval pottery dating from the 13th and 14th centuries. (1)

St Mary's Rickinghall Superior church dates from the 14th century, however the nave was rebuilt in the 15th century. The south porch with an upper chamber or parvise was added at this time, as was the parapet on the tower. Parvises were often where a chaplain or a chantry priest would live, later they were used to hold the documents and valuables belonging to the church. Arthur Mee, in his book about Suffolk from 1941 says that an old chest was found containing documents dating back to the 14th century in this parvise. The stairs to the parvise and the stairs to the rood loft are still in place. The stone seat running right around the inner wall of the nave was for the elderly and infirm as early medieval churches did not always have pews. This gave rise to the expression 'the weakest go to the wall'. The south west window in the chancel commemorates Samuel Speare, a village boy, who at the age of 15 went out to East Africa as a missionary. He died at the age of 20 in Lincolnshire in 1873 where he was being prepared to be ordained. (2) The carved octagonal font dates from the 14th century. The bier used to carry the coffins has the date 1763 and is similar to the one in Rickinghall Inferior church.

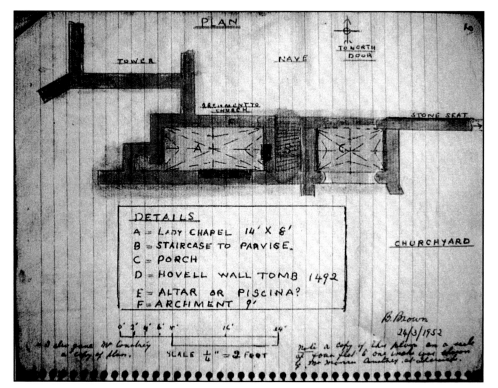

A page from Basil Brown's notebook showing details of the Lady Chapel

An unusual feature is a mason's mark that can be seen at the base of the outside of the tower on the south wall. There are six bells which are still rung by a group of bell ringers on Saturday mornings. In his will dated 1476 Thomas Hervy from Facons Hall left *'convenient & necessary timber for hanging 4 bells in the tower of Rekinghale Superior'*. (3) In Henry Elmy's Churchwarden's account for 1699 it is recorded that one shilling was paid for ringing the bells for the 'Gunpowder treason'. (4) An agreement exists from 1712 between John Goldsmith of Redgrave, a bell founder, and Churchwardens Michael Barnes and Henry Elmy to make five new bells. (5) Henry Elmy is buried in a table tomb grave in the churchyard on the north side of the church.

Beside the porch on the west side is an area where there was once a small lady chapel or chantry chapel. This was excavated in 1952 by Basil Brown who found that there appeared to have been a building measuring 14 feet x 6 feet 6 inches attached to the south porch on the west side. The entrance to this chapel is still visible on the south west wall of the nave where an arch can be seen and on the outside where the entrance has been blocked. In his will Thomas Hervy requested that he

17

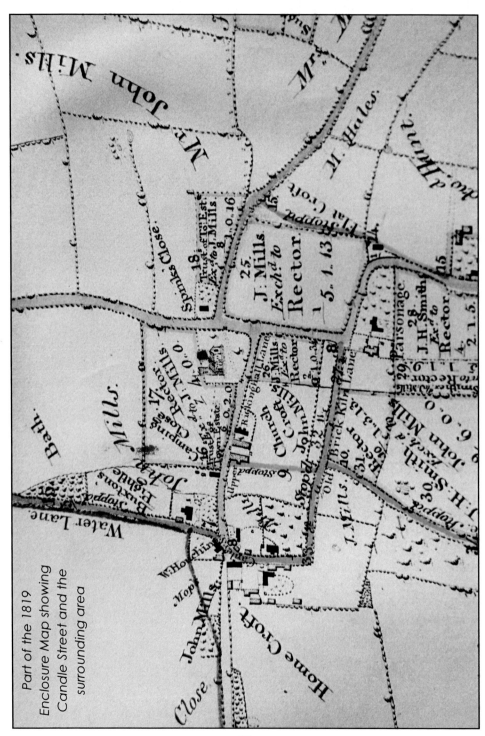

Part of the 1819
Enclosure Map showing
Candle Street and the
surrounding area

18

be *'buried in the chapel of St Mary annexed to the church of Rickinghall Superior'* (3) and in 1526 Thomas Sheppard left 6s 8d to the Lady Chapel. It is not known when this chapel was demolished or why. The church was declared redundant in 1977 and is now in the care of the Churches Conservation Trust.

The 1819 Enclosure Map shows a **'camping close'** in the field north west of the church running parallel with the present bypass. Camping or camp ball was a game something like football dating from the medieval period. It was played by any number of participants and could get very rough. It was often played between villages, as cricket is today.

Opposite the church, on the north corner of Church Lane where it meets the Finningham Road, is the site where it is thought the medieval **Gildhall** once stood. There were three gilds in Rickinghall Inferior and Superior: St John the Baptist, St. Peter and St Mary. These were not craft gilds but social gilds, more like friendly societies. In 1585 the field in which it stood was called Scouttis acre. A building which was possibly the old gildhall is visible on the 1819 Map but there is no sign of it today.

Kiln Farm Lane runs south of the church. It ends at Summer Lane which itself ends as a footpath leading to Briar Lane. However before it was closed in 1819 Summer Lane used to be a track leading to Allwood Green along the boundary between Rickinghall Inferior and Rickinghall Superior. The last part of this lane widened into a drift and it appears that it was at one time part of Allwood Green. The lane is recorded in a court roll from 1337 as 'Somerwey'. (6)

The houses situated near the church on either side of Kiln Farm Lane form the hamlet of Candle Street which now consists of four houses and the farmhouse with two converted barns. It is said that there was once a candle making business in the area which is why it is called Candle Street. The name Canler Street is on the 1819 Map. Canle is an old word for candle. In the early 20th century Candle Street was known as Water Lane. Until recently the cottages were owned by Falcon's Hall and were tied cottages, the tenants all working for Falcon's Hall Farm.

The first cottage on the left, the south side, is now called **1 & 2 Kiln Farm Cottages.** It was formerly divided into two but has recently been restored and is now one. It appears to date from the 17th century. Until recently none of the cottages along the lane had names or numbers. They did not need to as everyone knew where people lived!

The thatched cottages on the south side are now known as **3 & 4 Kiln Farm Cottages**. According to the listings this is a mid 16th century house which was extended in the 17th century. It was cased in Fletton bricks in the 19th century. In the early 20th century George Salter's family lived in number 4. In 1926 the Rush family moved to number 3 and lived there until the early 1960s when Mr & Mrs Sharman moved here and have lived here ever since.

The first cottage on the right (north side) is called **Kiln Cottage**. It is a thatched mid 17th century cottage. A 1918 sales document says it had 3 bedrooms, 2 sitting rooms and a kitchen. It is said to have been a beer house or pub at one time but there seems to be no record of this. The family of Richard Cook who died in the First World War lived here.

The next house on the right is **Cherry Tree House**. According to the listings it is a timber-framed house which was built about 1600. When it was sold in 1918 it was two dwellings. It was a smallholding of 2 acres 2 rods and appears to have been the only cottage in the lane which was not a tied cottage.

The footpath to the side of Cherry Tree House leads across the bypass and is the end of Water Lane. On the opposite side of the footpath there was a house, now demolished, in which Robert Silver lived in 1839. In the 18th century this was owned by William Houchin.   In 1865 Richard and Sophie Silver were accused of murdering two of their sons James and Charley. At an inquest held at The Bell they were both acquitted. James probably died from fungi poisoning although Charley may have died from arsenic poisoning.   Arsenic, used for removing fly on sheep, was found in a discarded bottle in a nearby field. *(7)*

Brick Kiln Farm, now called **Kiln Farm House**, is a 17th century timber-framed house which was extended in the 18th century. In 1839 it was owned by John Mills who at that time was leasing Facon's Hall Farm. The tenant farmer was George Porter and by 1844 his son William was the tenant. In a sales catalogue of 1918 it had a corn barn, bullock shed, granary, cart horse stable, bullock yard, cattle yard and horse yard. The two barns which probably date from the 18th century were converted into houses in the 1990s. They are now called **September Barn** and **Summer Barn**.

Further along Summer Lane there was a medieval thatched cottage. In the early 20th century this was lived in by Spencer Bailey, a stockman on the farm, then by his son Freddy Bailey who was the shepherd. The house became dilapidated and was burnt down to demolish it in the 1960s.

The brick kiln after which the farm is named was situated next to the wood beside the track which leads off to the right and runs between

Candle Street

Summer Lane and Briar Lane. It is not certain when this brick works first started making bricks but in 1839 it was being run by George Porter. In the 1930s there were still large piles of bricks beside the track but it appears that it had not been producing bricks for many years before that time.

Just beyond Kiln Farm Lane, as the **Finningham Road** turns sharply left is the **Parsonage** which was described in 1841 as '*small but remarkably neat and convenient, and contains four Bed Chambers, a Lumber Room, and Fruit Closet above; a good Parlour, Hall, Kitchen, Dairy, Washhouse and Pantry, with cellaring in the Basement*'.

A lane called Old Brick Kiln Lane used to go off to the right at this point, passing in front of the Parsonage and ending at Kiln Farm. It was closed in 1819.

To the left of the Parsonage stands **Highways**, formerly the Parsonage's tithe barn. It is an early 17th century barn which had a bungalow built inside the frame in 1954. At this time there was no access to the barn's upper area. In the early 1990s the present owners opened an access and converted the upper storey making three bedrooms. The principal rafters and the tie beams have sets of carpenters' marks; on the south side these are the usual Roman numerals, however on the north side they are a series of circles, which is very unusual indeed. It would be

interesting to see if any other buildings in the area have the same carpenters' marks. Today Highways is a smallholding selling meat from rare breed animals such as Gloucestershire Old Spot pigs raised on the premises.

Sunnyside is a nursery with a farm shop selling fruit and vegetables most of which are grown on the premises. The Mayhew family have farmed here since 1969.

Circular carpenters' marks
at Highways

Falcon's Hall used to be called Facon's Hall and was the site of the manor house of the Manor of Facons Hall. The earliest reference we have to this manor is in a document of 1284 when the son of William Talbot leased the Manor of Rickinghall to John and Maria Crowe. (8) It is not known where that manor house of Crowe's Hall stood; it could be near to the present day Suggenhall; however it is more likely to be on the site of Facon's Hall. In 1306 the Talbots still had possession of the manor but in 1305 Thomas Talbot had died and his widow Joan married Walter Faukoun. He appears in the 1327 Subsidy return for Rickinghall Inferior in which he pays 3s 6d, more than anyone else in either of the Rickinghalls. It seems that Facon's Hall took its name from this Walter Faukoun, although in the 15th century it was often still referred to as 'the manor of the Talbots'. After Joan died her son Peter Talbot succeeded to all her lands. In 1380 Edmund Talbot still retained the manor. (9) Sometime in the mid 15th century it came into the possession of Thomas Hervy who died in 1476. His son, also called Thomas, was in the service of Edward IV and by 1487 (after Henry VII had usurped the throne) he had 'no lands or chattels'. (9) It is probably at this time that the Tyrells of Gipping acquired the manor. There must have been bad feeling about this, for a court of enquiry in Ipswich in 1499 states that Thomas Hervy along with John and Simon Hervy and three others '*armed with sticks, swords, bills, daggers, bows & arrows riotously entered the Manor called Facons hall & expelled by force the said James Terell, knight.*' (10) This is probably the same James Tyrell who was Master of Horse to Richard III and who was later executed for the supposed murder of the 'Princes in the Tower'.

By 1507 the Yaxley family owned Facon's Hall. In 1525 Anthony Yaxley was accused of holding heretical views and there is a document of recantation signed by him. (10) However his grandson William was a recusant (someone who refused to give up the Catholic faith). In 1599

Anthony's son Henry sold the manor to Sir Nicholas Bacon. From then until the end of the 19th century it was owned by the lord of the manor and leased to tenant farmers. In a document dated 1620 William Rust leased the manor. The Rust family appear to have still occupied it in 1674 for in that year the Hearth Tax records William Rust as having eight hearths implying Facon's Hall was a large house. According to Edmund Farrer the families of Goate, Barnes, Maber and Mills followed the Rusts in leasing the farm; the last three appear to have been related by marriage. (10) In 1839 George Wilson was the owner and Noah Cook was the tenant farmer. In 1896 it came into the possession of the Barker family who still farm it today.

At the start of the drive is a pair of semi-detached houses built in the 19th century as farm cottages. The date stone on the front has '1890 GHW'. George Holt Wilson owned Falcon's Hall at the time.

Abbots Hall Farm which is situated on the left before reaching New Delight Road is actually in Botesdale where a tongue of land reaches down and ends at the Finningham Road. It appears to have belonged to the lord of the manor for many years. In a land indenture from 1612 in which Sir Nicholas Bacon leased it to Nicholas Gosse it was occupied by George Hasell. (11) Nan Hazle's Lane is a green lane which leads from this point up to Stubbing's Entry near Botesdale Common. It is not known who Nan Hazle was. She may have been a relation of George Hasell. However there may never have been a Nan Hazle; haysel is an old term for the haymaking season, perhaps this was a lane used to reach areas for hay making. In a lease dated 1696 the farm was leased to Thomas Flowerdew and had formerly been leased to William Tiptot. (12) The barn has a date stone '1844 G St V W' – George St Vincent Wilson was the lord of the manor at the time. In the early 20th century the Reynolds family were the tenant farmers.

In 1943 an American Fortress bomber crashed and caught fire in a field near Abbots Hall. All 10 crew members were killed. They had been trying to land at what they thought was an airfield but was in fact a decoy airfield at Burfields, which is not far from the farm.

Just beyond Abbots Hall there is a group of houses. The first one on the right is called **The Tiger.**

Thomas Middleton owned the land in 1819 but no house is shown on the Enclosure Map. In 1839 a house is shown on the Tithe Map so it is likely he had the cottage built. It was once a public house but so far the only reference to this is at the Petty Sessions reported in the Ipswich Journal for

12th April 1884 when the owner, John Thurston of Walsham, applied for an interim licence for it. It was reported that parishioners had petitioned for this licence not to be allowed as there was another public house within 50 yards of The Tiger. This must have been The Cross. Beer houses such as this one did not have a bar counter, merely a hatch to serve from, and there was a hatch between the kitchen and front room of The Tiger. The story goes that as it was a beer house it was not allowed to sell spirits. When the Customs and Excise men visited the spirits would be quickly taken across the road to Nan Hazle's Lane and hidden in the ditch!

The Mission Room was situated next to Crossways. It appears to have been built in the late 19th century. In 1899 a licence was granted for Revd George Hales to perform divine service there and for many years it was used by the parishioners of Allwood Green as it was nearer than Rickinghall Superior Church. However by the 1940s it was derelict. In 1946 the tiles and bricks were sold to Mr Goddard, the builder. Ken Rush was sent to remove these for reuse. After this the building was demolished.

Crossways was formerly a pub called The Cross and is situated at the cross-roads where New Delight Road meets the Finningham Road. It was owned by the Norwich Brewery, Youngs Cawshays and Youngs, and was built about 1880. The licensee in 1900 was Jonathan Baker. As with most other pubs in the villages a living could not be made from running the pub alone, so he was also a blacksmith. It closed as a pub in the 1950s. Rowland (Dodd) Tuffs was the last licensee. He was also a thatcher, mostly thatching the stacks of corn for the surrounding farms. Corn stacks had to be thatched, before the days of plastic, to keep the rain off.

Opposite these houses **Willow Farm** is now the Rickinghall Business Centre. The farm barn still survives and has been converted into offices.

Allwood Green is a very large former common where six parishes meet. These are Finningham, Walsham, Rickinghall Inferior and Superior, Gislingham and West Thorpe. The Botesdale boundary comes very close, meeting the Finningham Road at Abbots Hall. It also has the boundary between the Hartismere and Blackbourne Hundreds running through it. There appear to have been funnel-shaped extensions to the common at one time, extending towards Stubbings Entry beside Nan Hazle's Lane on the north east, towards Walsham-le-Willows on the south west, and along Summer Lane on the north. Each village would have the right to graze their animals on the common. There were gates to get onto the common at each entry point. In 1695 the Churchwardens paid 6 shillings for a 'sawn' gate to Allwood Green where Summer Lane joined it.

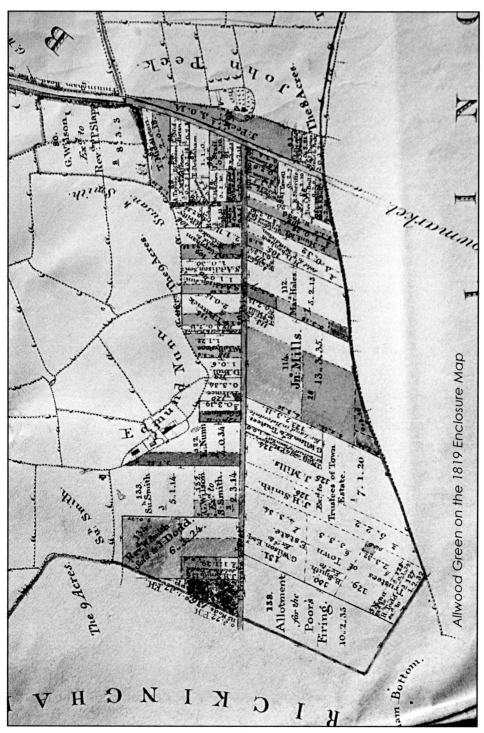

Allwood Green on the 1819 Enclosure Map

25

New Delight Road is a straight road running beside Allwood Green common. No one appears to know why it was called such a strange name but the story goes that when the road was being set out a straight line was ploughed to mark it. The ploughman was delighted at how straight it was, hence the name. It was always called common road by the people who lived there. It is exactly a mile long and apparently at one time pony and trap races would take place along it.

The Finningham part of the common had been enclosed in 1804 and it is thought that the Rickinghall side had started to be enclosed well before this date, probably in the mid to late 18th century. By 1819 it had been parcelled into 85 enclosures owned by about 35 different people. There are now several farms and cottages along this road most of which were built after 1819.

Most of the charity lands, such as the Rookewood Charity, the Poor's Firing Charity and the Town Lands were also situated along this road. These were usually pieces of land which had been left to the village, the rent from which went to the poor. Most of these lands were sold to private buyers in the early and mid 20th century. (13)

Cromwell's Plantation is a circular earthwork in the middle of Allwood Green in Finningham's part of the common. There is debate about when this was constructed and for what purpose. Often earthworks, such as this one, situated at the boundaries of villages were sites of Anglo-Saxon moots or assembly places. At an excavation in the 1930s Basil Brown found pottery which he thought dated to the Iron Age; however it is now thought to be 12th century. (14) Although earthworks such as this one are thought to be early Norman castles it is unlikely here. It has been suggested it could be a play place, where plays were performed, but as yet this is unsubstantiated. The name is not thought to be significant and probably only dates to the 19th century. At one time it was known as Fapes Hill (Fapes means gooseberry, a local dialect word) or Benny's Plantation after Benjamin Mulliner who lived in a cottage, called Stoland Abbey, on the site from the 1830s to the 1870s.

(1) SCC Sites and Monuments Record RKS 012 & 024 (2) See Quatrefoil book No.1 (3) Peter Northeast Gelour f177/8 & East Anglian Miscellany no:326 (4) SROI FB121 E1/4/1 (5) SROI FBA 121/E2/1/1 (6) SROI HA 240 2508/673 no.4 (7) Bury and Norwich Post August 1865 (8) PRO Feet of Fines CP25/1/215/36 (9) PRO Chancery Records C143/395/9 & C131/247/16 (10) East Anglian Miscellany no.8095 by Edmund Farrer (11) SROI HA 240/2508/16 (12) SROI HD 78 2671 (13) Parish Magazine June 2007 & April 2008 by Brian Chandler (14) Basil Brown & SCC Sites & Monuments Record FNN 005

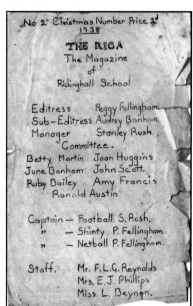

Part of the RICA Magazine - Editor Peggy Fellingham

The stream that goes under the road at the start of Hinderclay Road is called the **Swimming Ditch**. It runs from Water Lane under the road by Bridge House, past the church and under the Hinderclay Road. It then runs parallel with The Street until it eventually joins the stream running parallel to Lizzie's Lane in Botesdale.

There used to be a lane called **Love Lane** running parallel to the Swimming Ditch, approximately where the permissive footpath runs today. A cottage is shown beside it on the 1791 Glebe Map. In 1819 this belonged to W Cottingham but it appears to have been demolished by 1839. The lane crossed the top of the track leading from Fen Lane and then ran to the right of Broom Hills House, swinging round in front of what used to be called Fen Heads and later Paddlers Fen where there are fishing lakes today. It then became Fen Heads Lane. It eventually joined the Hinderclay Road just before it swings round to the right at the junction with Sparkes Lane. This lane was closed in 1819.

Beyond the churchyard on the left is **The National School** which was built in 1853 for £700 on glebe land donated by the Rector, the Revd Maul. The log books and other official documents about the school still survive. In 1939 some of the older students started a school magazine called The

Rica: so far we have only two copies but perhaps more will come to light. During the Second World War when evacuees arrived in the village the school was too small to accommodate them. Rickinghall Superior church was used as an annex and for a time the village children and the evacuees would go to the church for their lessons in alternate weeks. When most evacuees returned home the few remaining joined the village children at the school. The school finally closed in 1994 when the pupils were transferred to the purpose-built St Botolph's Primary School in Botesdale. The old school was converted into four private houses in 2006.

Lower Church Farm on the right was a working farm until the early 2000s. The farm buildings now have various businesses operating from them including R W Lister and Son, Motor Engineers.

The land for the **Village Hall** and playing fields was bought from John Holt Wilson in 1937 for £82 10s 0d and a management committee was formed. The original hall was an army Nissen hut which was erected in 1947. It used to have a small projector room reached by a ladder at the back. Films were put on weekly. The Youth Club also met once a week. The building was demolished when the present hall was built in the 1960s by local builders Bryant Brothers. This was extended several times in the 1990s. The skate park was built in 2005 and in 2008 the playground was rebuilt at a cost £35,000.

Some 450 events and meetings take place in the hall annually, among them the Farmers Market on the second Saturday of every month with a car boot sale in the summer months. Sporting events including football, netball and tennis take place on the multi-use games area and playing field. A cricket pavilion used to stand at the far end of the playing field. This had been moved from Barleybirch in Botesdale in 1949 and, having become dangerous, it was dismantled in 1982. A Vintage Car Rally was held here annually from 1977 until 2002, raising funds for the village hall, bowls club and other village charities and organisations.

Albert Close, a sheltered housing complex, is beyond the village hall and next to it on the left is a small estate of houses, called Church Meadow. Some of these houses are council houses built in 1947. Harry Goddard built them employing soldiers returning from the war. The wages for these men at this time were between 17/6d and £1 a week. Private houses facing the playing field were built in the late 1980s.

The ten houses on the right were completed in 2008. They were built as affordable homes by Circle Anglia in partnership with Mid Suffolk District Council.

Opposite Church Meadow is **Mill Lane**. The allotments on the right were established in 2009 and are for the inhabitants of both Rickinghall and Botesdale. Northfield Wood next to the allotments was established at the same time by Barwoods as woodland for the community. A circular space in the centre has fruit trees surrounding it and the rest of the area has been planted with trees native to the area.

'Wop' Garnham lived at **Keepers Lodge** after he retired. He was the gamekeeper at Redgrave Hall before and after the Second World War. He would allow the boys to help with 'brushing' when there was a shoot. They were paid for this and would also be given a brace of pheasants.

A mill was situated on the right of the lane in a field before reaching Mill House and Cottage. It was probably on this site as early as 1608 as there is reference to free land with a windmill in the survey of this date. At this time the miller was Barnabus Bronde who paid a rent of 2d annually to the lord of the manor. In 1641 Thomas Howlett owned it and again paid rent of 2d. In 1747 Mary Largent paid rent for the land 'with a mill built upon it' which had belonged to her brother William. Again the rent was 2d so it had not increased in 150 years. (1) The mill appears on the 1791 Glebe Map and on the 1819 Enclosure Map when John Nunn was the owner. In 1839 Daniel Walton was the owner and the miller was John Wiseman. It was still standing in 1884 when it was sold to Samuel Robinson of the malting and milling family who owned several mills in Rickinghall and Botesdale. Perhaps he had it demolished as it does not appear on the 1905 Ordnance Survey Map. (2)

Mill House and **Mill Cottage** were built in about 1800 as the home for the miller.

A little further on, a footpath leads off to the left from Mill Lane towards Hinderclay Road. Just before the road the path goes through an area called Mill Mount on the Enclosure Map. It is thought that this is where the medieval mill called Brommelle (Broom Mill) was situated. Many medieval documents refer to it. It was a working mill as early as 1340, probably earlier. In the Redgrave manor account roll for 1340 under the heading 'Cost of the mills' it says '*In the stipend of 4 carpenters for 4 days for the mill called le Brommelne ... to the same 3s 8d for each day 11d.*' Carpenters usually seemed to receive 3d a day at this time so this was slightly less. (3) In 1351 the mill was leased for 26s 8d for the year. (4) This mill was probably demolished when the new one was built near the present Mill Lane in the 17th century. There is some dispute as to where the old mill was as no trace of it has been found when ploughing on this site. However as it would have been built of wood on an earth mound it would be difficult to find very much evidence without doing an archaeological excavation. Perhaps air photography will resolve this.

At one time Mill Lane only went as far as the Mill House but it was extended in the 20th century.

Broomhills is, according to the Revd Edmund Farrer, a 16th century house which was extended and faced with brick in the 18th century. (5) In the early 18th century the Barnes family owned it. In his will of 1741 Joseph Barnes left Broomhills to Michael and Elizabeth Barnes, his father and mother, who were farming there at the time. (6) It was acquired by the Holt family in the late 18th century and in an estate survey of 1849 J.C Burroughes the tenant farmer was paying rent of £124 per annum. In that year it is described as having a *'Nag stable and harness house, cart stable, cowhouse with calf pens and a range of piggeries'*. An agreement exists between George Holt Wilson and the farm bailiff, John Sage, from October 1880 which says he was to receive a weekly wage of £1 for the services of himself and his wife. He did have other allowances. For instance for every chicken or duck reared he received 3d. In the early 20th century the Wilson family used the house as a residence. 'Bromhills' is referred to in the 1289 extent and the name 'le Brom' is mentioned in many of the medieval documents but it is not clear where the house stood at that time.

In the 1960s Basil Brown did an excavation in a field nearby which produced evidence that the area had been occupied from the Neolithic period. He interpreted the site as a Saxon manor house built on a Neolithic causewayed camp. (7) He encouraged the local children to help him and there is a list of these children, each having signed their name in his notebooks.

Returning to **Hinderclay Road** there are two new bungalows on the left: Oak Lodge built in 2001 and The Spinney built in 1996. **East Lodge** is at the entrance to Snape Hill House drive. It was probably built in the 19th century.

Snape Hill House was formerly known as Hill House and in the late 18th century and early 19th century as 'The Mansion House'. It is a 17th century house which was altered in about 1820 by the Amys family who lived here until 1842 when C J Norton, an architect, purchased it from them. (8) In the 1870s he rebuilt and enlarged the existing house adding a third storey and a 'French turret' to one side. (7) This led to it being called the 'pill box' by local people. The farm buildings that date from the 18th century are still standing. The house and farm were bought by the Holt Wilson family in 1909. They lived here from the 1950s to the 1980s.

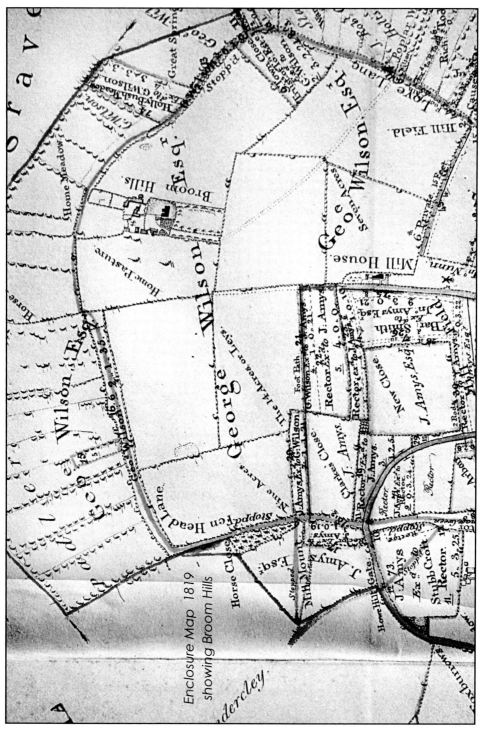

Enclosure Map 1819 showing Broom Hills

31

Snape Hill House with turret and balustrade

The next drive is to **The Old Rectory**, the home of the rectors of Rickinghall Inferior until the early 1970s. In a sales catalogue from 1841 it was described as being in the 'cottage style' however at this time it had six 'good bedchambers' a drawing room, dining room, kitchen and a range of farm and outbuildings. It was extended and re-fronted in 1850 by Revd Maul. There are stones in the garden which appear to be medieval. They were possibly removed from the church when it was restored in the 1850s.

A footpath called Parsonage Road used to lead from the Rectory south to join the Hinderclay Road near Mill Lane. Going north it passed through Parsonage Green crossed the Hinderclay Road and became Fen Head Lane. This was closed in 1819. The Hinderclay Road swings round sharply to the right and at this point the lane called Sparkes Lane leads off to the left. This area was called Howe Hill, one of the highest points in the area. Howe comes from the Viking haugr meaning hill. (9)

(1) HA 240/2508/1013 1747 Fo:44v (2) Old Bakery deeds (3) BL Add Roll 63372 (4) Bacon 337 (5) East Anglian Miscellany 1926 no:7306 & IRO HD 78 2671 (6) SROI HA 240/2508/1013 fo:22(7) Basil Brown notebooks (8) SROI HA 240/2508/1492 (9) Millennium Miscellany p.78

Chapter 5 The Street to Inglenook Cottage North Side

Church Farm House and **Church Cottage** is a late 15th century timber-framed building. It has a jetty with a dragon post on the corner. The Revd Thomas Peyton Slapp owned it in the first half of the 19th century and Isaacher Warren was the tenant farmer. It is now divided into two dwellings. In the late 19th and early 20th century Basil Brown's father farmed here and Basil lived here until the 1930s. A fire hook was always kept on the wall beside the house. In the event of fire in a thatched building these hooks were used to pull the thatch off to stop the fire spreading. They were often kept in the porch of churches. This fire hook is now in the Ipswich museum. In the 1970s Church Farm Cottage was leased by Canadian artist Michel DesRochers, who painted many views of the church.

The barn associated with Church Farm, **Church Farm Barn**, was converted into two dwellings in the 1980s. These form a T shape and the Swimming Ditch flows underneath the back section. The barn appears to have been built in the early 18th century but was enlarged in 1792. This date is on one end of the building, the initials I M are on the other. It is probable that these initials stand for John Mills who owned the land and barn at this time. A bungalow behind Lamorna is built on the site of the farm's old horse pond.

The **Old Post Office** and **Lamorna** was one medieval building. In the 19th century the roof was raised in the Old Post Office. There are two medieval 'service doors' in the Old Post Office and apparently there is a crown post roof in Lamorna. These indicate that it is an early building probably dating from the late 15th century. In a medieval house service doors led into the buttery and pantry from the cross passage. The cooking would have been done on a fire in the centre of the main room of the house called the hall. Sometime later in the 16th century a fireplace and chimney would have been inserted at one end of the hall where the cooking would then be done. The cross passage appears to be where the front door is today.

In 1839 the owner of both houses was William Battley, a shopkeeper from Redgrave. The tenant was John Foulger. In 1830 a John Folger was a chemist and druggist, so it could be the same person. (1) In the early 20th century Miss Self ran a general grocery shop here. (2) It appears the Post Office moved across from Lavender Cottage in the late 1930s. Mr Stone had the shop and Post Office at this time. Mr & Mrs Harry Chard took over both from him. Both were closed in 1985 when they retired. In the 1960s the Bryant Brothers found a large, possibly medieval, water pot in

The school garden plots

the garden of Lamorna when digging a drainage pit. Basil Brown was brought in to identify the pot which is now in Ipswich Museum.

Little Patches is a modern house on the site of the Rickinghall School garden allotments. Each boy from Rickinghall School had his own 'little patch' to garden. (The girls were taught sewing). The story goes that in the 1940s and 1950s the headmaster Mr. (Flogger) Reynolds would bring the boys to their patches then go to the White Horse for a beer while they worked. It appears that Flogger got his name not from his readiness to use the cane, but because his initials were FLGR.

Baylees and **Hazel Cottage** are a pair of cottages built in the 19th century.

Old Timbers and **Flint Cottage** are 17th century semi-detached cottages which were re-fronted with knapped flint in the early 19th century. The Francis family lived in Flint Cottage in the 20th century. Charles Francis died in the Second World War and his name is on the War Memorial.

The cottage now known as **Margaret Cottage** is where Mr. Bullock the builder and undertaker had his business in the mid 20th century. The two next door cottages, **Rose Cottage** and **Vine Cottage** were also part of his business. The workshop was derelict when Mr & Mrs Clark, the last owners, converted it into a dwelling. They called it Margaret Cottage after their Australian daughter-in-law. She died young and they wished to remember her in this way.

The Street
Note The Chequers sign and Robinson's malting in the background

Old Chequers dates from the mid to late 16th century. The listing says it was extended in the mid 17th century and the fireplace has the date of 1652 on it. It was an inn in the early 20th century but before that it was probably a beer house. In 1918 George 'Joe' Whistlecraft was charged at the Ixworth Petty Sessions for breaking windows at The Chequers. It was owned by Youngs Brewery at that time and Mr Leathers was the landlord. (3) Frank Pearce whose sons Maurice and Ronald died in the Second World War was landlord here in the 1930s. It is now a private house.

Cob Tree Cottage, Tudor Oak Cottage, Hunnypot Cottage and Tudor Cottage are in a row which used to be known as Widows Row. In the 19th and early 20th century these were, apparently, divided into as many as eight cottages and because they were very small, although not alms houses, widows tended to live here hence the name. Cob Tree Cottage and Tudor Oak Cottage probably date to the early 16th century. Some of the roof timbers were found to have soot on them which suggests a hall house. A chimney stack and back-to-back fireplace were inserted at a later date. There are carpenters' marks on the upstairs timbers of Tudor Oak Cottage. There are also many 'taper burns'. These marks are not accidental; they were deliberately burnt onto the timber because superstition at the time meant people thought this would be protection against fire. Hunnypot and Tudor Cottage were built in the 19th century to form the row. A brick building behind the cottages is probably

Robinson's malting was demolished in 1926.
Jubilee House stands here now.

another cottage or perhaps a wash house for all the cottages.

It is thought that this is where Samuel Speare's family lived in the mid 19th century. He was the boy who went as a missionary to East Africa for five years in the 1860s and 1870s and died in 1873 at the age of twenty. A window in the Upper Church is dedicated to him.

The Chestnuts was formerly a field called Malting or Accommodation Meadows. The houses here were built in the late 1980s.

Jubilee House stands on the land where Robinson's Maltings once stood. In 1839 James Smith was the maltster here. A sales catalogue dated 24th February 1910 describes the maltings as having a frontage of 174 feet to the street and that it comprised *'Two Steeps, with good water supply, 3 Pavement and Cement Working Floors, and a total area of 7000 square feet. Two Drying Kilns, 27-ft by 24-ft and 23-ft by 21-ft respectively, lately rebuilt upon modern principle, with pitch pine lined roofs & ventilators, and fitted with overhead tram rails for loading and unloading. Two Furnaces and large coal stores. Extensive Malt and Barley Stores, each to hold about 3000 Coombs and a chive Chamber'*. In the First World War the Maltings were used by soldiers as a canteen. Maltings were often requisitioned by the army as they were large open spaces. The Maltings complex was demolished in March 1926; this was documented by Edmund Farrer who took photographs at the time. The house was built in 1935 and named Jubilee House as it was the Silver Jubilee of King George V that year. In the 1940s and 1950s the Misses Warren had their school here. It consisted of two rooms in the house. The whole class would be taught sitting around one long table.

Jubilee House Barn is behind Jubilee House and is an 18th century former stable block to the maltings. It was recently renovated and is now a dwelling called **The Nettis.**

Maltings Cottages were built in the 18th century as part of the Maltings complex which stood next to them. In the same sales catalogue in which the Maltings were being offered for sale it says '*Also adjoining is a Double Cottage, one tenement containing Two Sitting Rooms, Kitchen with copper, Pantry and Two Bedrooms, and the other Sitting Room and Bedroom; together with Sheds, Closets and Gardens, and (are) occupied by Mrs. Smith and Edward Bailey, at rents producing £7 12 0 per annum*'. In the 1980s the then owner Mrs Viel had her cottage 'stone clad'. Mid Suffolk District Council served an enforcement order on her to have the cladding removed as it had been done without permission. However as she was in her 90s it was allowed to remain. It was removed at a later date when the cottage was renovated. (4)

Two sets of semi-detached cottages are dated to the 18th century. **The Old Four Horse Shoes** and **Beame Cottage** are the first two, followed by **Honeysuckle Cottage** and **Inglenook Cottage** (previously called Wynville). The Four Horse Shoes is a flint faced cottage which was sold in 1719 by William Houchin. In 1823 it was described as a dwelling house and blacksmith's shop. In 1868 it became a beer house and continued as such until the early 20th century. In the mid 20th century it was David Bailey's dairy farm and was at that time called Street Farm. The Bailey family appear to have lived in this cottage from at least 1839 when Charles Bailey was the tenant. He was still the tenant in 1850.

(1) Pigot's Directory 1830 (2) Millennium Miscellany P.91 (3) Diss Express 13.9.1918 (4) East Anglian Daily Times

The house now called **Breklaw** was a shop in 1839 when it was owned by John Davis who rented it to William Jackson. It had probably been a shop for many years before this. It was called The Corner Shop for much of the 20th century. In the 1920s and 30s Kate Davey, a 'confectioner' and grocer, had her business here. The Marshall family had a grocers and drapers shop in the mid 20th century which they sold to the Rugman family in 1972. It was a Craft Shop run by Gerald and Barbara Walker from 1987 until 2003.

Rossendale was possibly in the same tenement as Breklaw. In the late 17th century Robert Randall had the copyhold. In 1839 it was owned by William Lillystone with Benjamin Bennett occupying the premises. In the 1830 Pigot's Trade Directory he was advertised as a baker so perhaps this was a bakery with a shop at this period. In 1936 it was agreed by the Parochial Church Council (PCC) that they needed a Parish Room and they decided to rent the house for 7s 6d per week. It was decided that members over 18 years should pay a subscription of 1s 3d a quarter or 5s a year, those between 16 and 18 years paid 1s a quarter or 4s a year. It is thought this arrangement only lasted until 1939. (1) Mr & Mrs Shaw had an antique shop here in the 1980s.

Linden House was formerly called The Garden Plot. Although the deeds date from 1742, which is probably when the present house was built, there appears to have been a house standing on the site earlier which may have been called Oakham. In the court books for 1706 Jonathan Debenham took over the copyhold from John Sparkes and Elizabeth his wife. At this time there appears to have been a shop as well as a house on the site. In 1750 it was sold to Isaac (a wool comber) and Elizabeth Bennett, who left it to Mary Farrow. The Farrow family held the copyhold until 1852 when Robert Freeman bought it. His family held it until 1921. (2) The house was called Lime House until the 1980s when it was changed by Major Clarke the then owner to Linden House as his wife was German and Linden is the German for Lime.

Forge Cottage is an early 16th century timber-framed thatched house which had a chimney stack inserted in the 17th century. There is a Phoenix fire insurance plaque on the front wall. In the 17th century William Rust held the tenement and by the 1740s it had passed to Thomas Slapp and Ann his wife. The Revd Peyton Slapp still owned part of the tenement in 1839. It was occupied at this time by Isaacher Warren who was the tenant farmer at Church Farm. The Shemming family lived here in the early 20th century.

Herbert Shemming and later his son Frank (Harry) were blacksmiths for many years from the 1890s until the 1930s. Their forge was in a building along the street between Tiger Cottage and the house now called **Shemmings**, which is where Bob Shemmings, Herbert's grandson, lived in the later 20th century. Herbert and Ellen's son Robert came back from Canada to serve in the First World War. He died in 1918 and his name is on the War Memorial. To the left of the house are the remains of a Second World War pill box. In the 1830s and 40s Thomas Patrick senior and his son Thomas Patrick junior were blacksmiths on this site.

Tiger Cottage and **Forge Close** are two cottages forming an L shape. Tiger Cottage, which used to be called The Forge, dates from the late 16th century and is a lobby entrance house which fronts onto the street. Forge Close is at the back forming an L with Tiger Cottage. The listings say it was possibly built in the 18th century.

Between Tiger Cottage and Benrosa there used to be a small thatched timber-framed cottage known as Brown's because Arthur Brown had lived there. It was condemned and demolished in the 1970s.

Harveys Close is on the site of Shepherd's Bus Company. The Shepherds had a carriers business here from the 1890s and also offered cabs for hire. In the 1930s they had cars for hire and Edward Shepherd was a 'motor bus proprietor'. The business was sold to Simonds' Bus Company of Botesdale in 1935. The Shepherd family lived at what is now called **Lavender Cottage**, recently Green Cottage. It was the Post Office which was run from the early 20th century until the 1930s by Mrs Shepherd and after her by Miss Eliza Shepherd. A photograph from the early 20th century shows this house with advertisements for Castrol oil and cars for hire.

Hall House and **Tipplers** are in one building which according to the listing is a 15th century house, originally one house of five bays with a two bay open hall. When it was listed in 1988 the roof had smoke-blackened rafters, which indicates that this was an open hall house. In the early 17th century a chimney was added and a floor was put into the hall area so adding a second storey. The deeds only go back to 1710 when the owners were John and Dinah Ellis, but by 1753 and for the rest of the 18th and 19th century the house appears to have been divided into three dwellings. For much of this time it was owned by the Freeman and Mills families who owned land throughout the villages. In the late 19th century a wheelwright had his business here. There was a cart house on the premises where carts were repaired. In the early 20th century the east end of Tipplers had a single storey extension to which an upper storey has now been added. In 1990 a fire burnt much of the thatched roof and upper floors of both dwellings but luckily much of the timber frame survived.

A cottage between The Old Bakery and Tipplers was at one time a shoemakers shop. It was demolished in 1954.

The Old Bakery was possibly built in the 18th century although the earliest house record is for 1811. However a chamfered principal joist with a stop suggests the oldest part of the building could date from the 17th century. It was originally part of the White Horse pub and belonged to the Robinson family in the late 19th century. It was part of an estate which included the mill in Mill Lane, Rickinghall. The Matthews family were tenants here from 1907. They bought the house in 1927 and it was a bakery from that time. In the 'Millennium Miscellany' Mrs Hunter remembers as a child taking their Sunday lunch to be cooked at the bakery. (3) In 1940 a British bomber crashed into the field opposite after colliding with electric cables. The pilot tried to fly between the houses but as it flew over a wing knocked a chimney off the house. The pilot and navigator were killed, but the wireless operator survived. There was strict security at the time so nothing appeared in the newspapers.

The White Horse public house is an early 17th century house with an attached 18th century kitchen and brewhouse. It is possible that the business moved from the Market Place in Botesdale in the late 18th century as there had been an inn of that name there for many years in the building now occupied by The Greyhound pub. Early references to a White Horse inn could be to either Botesdale or Rickinghall so it is difficult to know to which they are referring. Even recently The Greyhound has been said to be in Rickinghall. The pub was definitely here by 1825 as it is named in the Tippler's deeds. In 1830 Robert Freeman is mentioned as the landlord. In 1839 Robert Sheriffe of Sheriffe Brewery was the owner and John Greengrass was the licensed victualler. In 1840 when the Sheriffe Brewery was selling the premises it was described as having a 'large trade in wines, spirits and beer'. It had a spacious club-room, a parlour, bar-parlour, large kitchen with cellars and stabling for nine horses.

The White Horse

(4) In the 1840s Henry Rednall was the publican. It has been a pub since then and is still in business today.

North View is made up of four separate dwellings in one building. This was built of clay lump, brick and flint in the 19th century. It is a three-storied building, with a back extension to numbers 3 and 4. Walter Rednall bought the whole building in 1894. He was a builder and it is possible that it was he who added this extension. The top floor was once used as a dormitory by workers from the malting across the road. In 1933 Mr Francis, a tailor, purchased all four cottages and extensively renovated them, adding a side extension to number 4 to act as his workshop. Matilda Chenery was the tenant of Number 1 for many years. She lived there with her six children, two of whom, Edward and Oliver, were killed in the First World War.

Stanwell House is a late 18th century building which was brick fronted in the early 19th century. Mrs Hall lived here for many years in the early 20th century. She gave out Coronation Mugs to the local children in 1911. In the 1930s and 40s the girls from Rickinghall School were sent to Miss Carpenter, who lived there at that time, for sewing lessons. She also taught them cookery and household management.

The cottage formerly Marionora and now called **Daisy Cottage** has the hairdressers, Cut Above, in the building extension to the left. The extension was recently Ted Smith's electrical shop and before that was Masterson's electrical shop, prior to which it was a butchers shop for many years, firstly owned by Mr Howard then Mr Ostler. At the start of the First World War the cottage was owned by a retired army captain, possibly Captain Carman, who used his front room as a recruiting office where Rickinghall men went to join up.

L. T. Howard Butchers, now Daisy Cottage

41

The terrace of four cottages, now three, known as **Chestnut View, Meadow View** and **Glenfield** was built in 1851, by James King, in front of an older range of buildings and a small house called the **Whitings**, which have now been demolished. In 1851 the cottage now known as Glenfield was a butchers shop run by James King. In 1926 Rosetta Fellingham took out a lease on Glenfield and opened a sweet and tobacco shop. She bought all the

cottages in 1933 for £295. Fire insurance at that time was four shillings (20p) a year. She ran the shop for over 40 years finally closing it in 1971 when decimal coinage was introduced. Her husband Jim ran a poultry business from a building in the yard at the back. (5) In the 1970s two of the cottages were knocked into one to make the larger cottage now known as Chestnut View.

Rosetta Fellingham with daughter Peggy, in front of the sweet shop

White Gate is an early 17th century lobby entrance house, part of which was rebuilt in the 18th century. In 1890 it was owned by Henry Rednall, who had several properties in the village, and occupied by Isaac Debenham described as a herbalist.

In the mid 20th century there were two small buildings in the garden of White Gate. A fish and chip shop, owned by Tom Shaw, was situated in a wooden building approximately where **Mayberry House** is today. The fish and chips were cooked on a coal fire and were, according to many reports, extremely good. Mr Shaw was originally a fish merchant who in 1933 rented one of the cottages in the Glenfield terrace. There was a small brick building where **Bygones** is situated today. In the 1930s this had been a sweet shop but after the war it became an antique shop called 'Bygones'.

The fish & chip shop was housed in the wooden building

Redholme was formerly two cottages. 'WS 1862' is on a date stone on the side of the building. This is probably the date when the two cottages were made into one house and brick faced. Possibly 'WS' is William Street, who owned other houses in the area in the 1860s. In the 20th century a railway carriage was situated in the garden to the left of Redholme. This was owned by Charles Birk who was a boot and shoe maker and had his shop there. The carriage was removed in 1984 and is now in the Transport Museum at Carlton Colville near Lowestoft.

Walsingham Mews was built in the late 1980s. From the medieval period until the 19th century the stray animal pound was situated on the corner of this site. It appears on

Charles Birk's boot & shoe shop

a sales document map dated 1850. In the 1920s George Tacon Chapman had a garage and cycle repair shop on the site. (6) Billy Walsingham bought the garage in the 1930s. It remained a garage until the 1980s when the then owner Mr Johnson sold it for redevelopment. 'Ossie' Simonds worked here until starting his own garage and coach business in Botesdale in the 1930s. The house associated with the garage was behind the garage in Garden House Lane.

(1) Minute Book Rickinghall PCC 1923-1936 (2) House deeds (3) Millennium Miscellany p.97 (4) Sales Catalogue in Diss Museum (5) From an article by Chris & Marcia Bell (6) Kelly's Directory 1925.

George Tacon Chapman's Garage

The Garden House about 1920. The pub closed some 10 years earlier

In the medieval period **Garden House Lane** was known as Patlot way. At this time the large field on the left beyond Ryder's Way was known as Patlot Field. In the 17th and 18th centuries the Howchin (or Houchen) family owned this field and from then until the mid 20th century it was called Howchin's Field. The field next to it, which is now on the other side of the bypass, was formerly known as The Frith. In medieval times it was a large wood – frith is an early word meaning a wooded area.

Willow Cottage is a late 17th early 18th century cottage which had been divided into two. Basil Brown thought that it may have been owned by the Howchin family at this time. In the 19th century it was owned by James Hamblin Smith and when he died in 1850 it was put up for sale. At that time it was in the occupation of William Huggins and was described as *'A substantial cottage and carpenter's shop and a neat garden in front'*. A second shop was unoccupied. In 1880 Charles Silver purchased the *'cottage in two tenements with a neat garden in front'*. Miss True lived in the cottage from 1967 until the late 1990s. While the roof was being re-thatched in the 1980s an unexploded incendiary bomb was discovered in the thatch. It had failed to go off when dropped during the Second World War and had been there ever since. (1)

In the 1830s and 40s John Crack, a tailor and his wife Rebecca occupied the cottage now known as **The Walk**. Charles Silver bought the house in the 1880s. In 1910 it was occupied by Eliza Fiske and at that time comprised a living room and two bedrooms. The Foulger family have lived in the extended cottage since the 1950s.

Wheatfields housing estate off to the right was built in the late 1980s. The housing estate on the left is called Ryders Way and is named for Dr Ryder Richardson who was the doctor for the villages for many years. There is also a Basil Brown Close on this estate.

Lilac Cottage appears to be an 18th century house which was at one time divided into two dwellings. In 1850 these were occupied by Jonathan Silver and Widow Alecock. Another cottage between Lilac Cottage and Garden House was demolished in the early 20th century.

Garden House is a 16th century building, possibly a hall house, which was extended and altered in the early 17th century. From the 18th century until the early 20th century it was a pub called The Gardenhouse Inn. In 1839 Henry Debenham was the owner and it was occupied by James Gooderham. At this time it had a bowling green behind the building. Thomas Chapman was the landlord in 1844 and in 1855 James Bailey was the licensed victualler. By 1874 John Last was the landlord and Thomas Chapman was again landlord in 1884. (2) In the 1901 Census the landlord Joseph Westly described himself as 'Innkeeper & molecatcher'. Most pub landlords at this time had to have a second occupation to help make ends meet. By the 1920s it had ceased to be a pub and had

Basil Brown working in a trench in Cook's Field

45

become a private house. Mr & Mrs Grainger bought the house from Mr Smith in the 1930s.

In the mid 20th century Basil Brown excavated an area near Kiln House, in part of what used to be called Cooks Field. He discovered Roman kilns with a workshop nearby. Rickinghall, Wattisfield and Hinderclay appear to have been busy industrial areas in the Roman period with kilns found in many different places around the villages.

Garden House Lane crosses the bypass and becomes a footpath leading to Church Lane, at one time called Suggenhall Lane. Archaeological test pits and field walking carried out when the bypass was built in the mid 1990s record some medieval pottery at this point but little else. (3) The footpath joins the road at the junction of Church Lane and Potters Lane. To the right at this point is Suggenhall Farm.

The listing for **Suggenhall** says it is a 17th century house which was extended in the 19th century. However it appears that there had been a building on this site for many years before this. The first reference to 'Sugenhale' that has been found so far is in a document recording fines paid to the lord of the manor in the 13th and 14th centuries. In the year 1289 it is recorded that *'Matylda Sugenhale gave the lord 12d for her licence to marry Walter Spareche'*. (4) At this early date surnames were literal; usually being either 'occupational' (for instance someone with the surname Carpenter was a carpenter) or 'locative' which indicated where a person lived or came from (Nicholas Lopham came from Lopham). In this case 'Sugenhale' is a locative surname and it suggests that Matilda must have lived at or in the Suggenhall area. In which case there must have been a Suggenhall in Rickinghall at this early date. The next reference is from the 1437 extent of the manor. It records that Richard Coupere and his wife Beatrix held land *'lying in the place called Sogenhale'*. Documents from the 16th century onwards record that the Tiptott family held Suggenhall for over a century from approximately the 1540s until at least 1656. (5) In the 1608 extent John Typtott held a building at Suggenhall grene. The 1819 map shows Suggen Hall Green next to the house. After this Thomas Fitling leased it for several years. An indenture from 1673 survives naming him as the occupier. (6) In the Hearth Tax of 1674 he is noted to have five hearths so it must have been a large house. In the 1673 Indenture he and William Browne leased to John Browne all the *'Capytall Messuage or Tenement called Suggenhal House in which the said Thomas Fitling now dwelleth & wherein Thomas Hunt did late dwell situate lyinge & Beyng in Upper Rickinghall aforesaid with all & singular the barns stables houses yards orchards'*. It appears the Browne family owned the land from 1685 until at least 1745 when Peregrina the

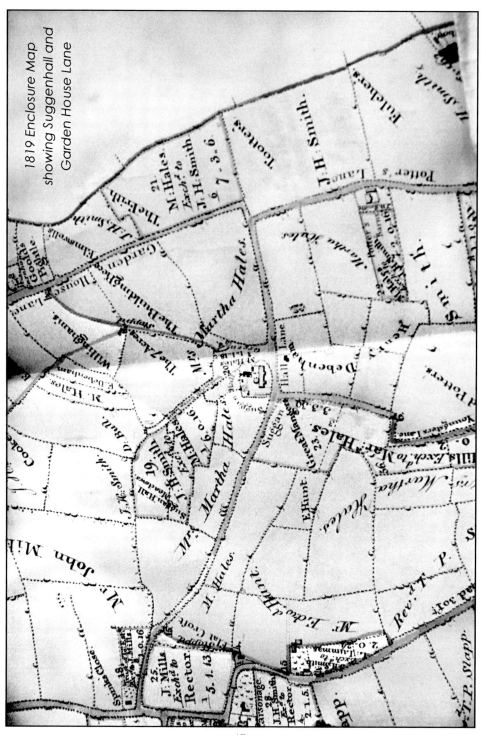

1819 Enclosure Map showing Suggenhall and Garden House Lane

47

wife of John Browne's grandson, another John Browne, died leaving all the land to their three sons. (7)   In 1819 Martha Hales owned the house and land. In 1839 the house and land were owned by Henry Buck but occupied by John Newton. From about 1841 until 1911 the Newstead family were tenant farmers here. In 1919 the Brown family (not related to the earlier family) bought it and have owned it ever since. Suggenhall Barn was converted into a dwelling in 2005.

It has been thought that Suggenhall could be the site of Crowe's Hall manor, held by John and Mary Crowe referred to in documents from the late 1200s. However the fact that Matilda Sugenhale was named in 1289 suggests that Suggenhall was a messuage with a hall in its own right by then. It is possible that Crowe's Hall was in fact the first name for Facon's Hall.

Church Lane turns right into **Potters Lane** and **Potters Farm** is on the right. In the early 1800s this was owned but not occupied by James Hamblin Smith. It was sold with his other properties after his death in 1850. A sales document from that date describes the farm as having a tiled cottage, barn, stable, cart lodges and shelter sheds along with 76 acres of arable and pasture. (8)

Just beyond Potters Farm is a wooded area where the Second World War **Observer Post** stood. There is anecdotal evidence that in the 19th century a cottage on the site was used as a pest house or isolation unit. In 1942 the land was let to the Air Ministry and the brick observation post was built. Until the end of the war it was manned 24 hours a day, 7 days a week in four-hour shifts by members of the Botesdale Royal Observer Corps made up of local residents, among them Basil Brown and Peggy Fellingham. Peggy was allowed to join just before her 18th birthday in 1942. There were four posts in the group at Diss, Stradbroke, Debenham and Botesdale. They were linked by telephone to one another and to a control centre in the Guildhall in Bury St Edmunds. Botesdale and Debenham allowed women to be part of the group but Diss and Stradbroke did not. The brick structure had already been completed by the time Peggy joined in November 1942. There was a platform on top of the post upon which a machine for estimating the height of the aircraft was situated. This was reached by steps on the outside. The observers became adept at recognising aircraft engine sounds and could pick out enemy engines even when amongst allied aircraft.

In 1956 an underground monitoring post was built here. It was used until 1968 when the site was returned to Rickinghall Parish Council. This has now been sealed, the brick tower demolished and an information board placed on the site. (9)

Botesdale Common (formerly called Micklewoodgreen) used to have gates at every entry point. In the 1694 Churchwarden's Account 6d was paid for a hook for 'Micaelwodgreen' gate. (10)

(1) Newspaper article, perhaps the Diss Express, & Basil Brown's Notebook No.LIV p.2. (2) Kelly's 1844, 1855 and Whites Directories. (3) SCC sites and Monuments Record RKS 025 (4) BL Add 40063 fo:10v (5) 1608 & 1656 surveys IRO HA 240 2508 1466 & 145 & 1543 BL Add 40063 (6) SROI HA 240/2508/324 (7) SROI HA 240/2508/1013 (8) Redgrave Estate Documents No:269(9) Interview with Peggy Healey (née Fellingham), 22 Feb 2004 & The Heritage Circle Magazine Winter 2009/2010 by Brian Chandler (10) SROI FB121 E1/4/1

MICKLEWOOD GREEN

(Adjacent to Botesdale Common)

Observation Post

The above photographs show the Observation Tower built in 1943 and from this high point enemy aircraft could be tracked as they swept in along the Waveney Valley on their way to bomb East Anglian Airfields.

The post was manned 24 hours a day throughout the war by local residents.

The photo on the left shows the insignia worn by Members of the Royal Observer Corps. The design was taken from an Elizabethan drawing of 'Beacon Watchers' with the motto 'Forewarned is Forearmed'

This plaque has been placed here by
Rickinghall Parish Council
to commemorate the Observation Tower built in 1943
and used by the Royal Observer Corps
in the defence of this country until 1968

- March 2003 -

History

EXTRACT FROM THE RICKINGHALL SUPERIOR INCLOSURE AWARD OF 1819:

The award or Instrume t in writing of John Josselyn of Sproughton in the County of Suffolk Gentleman the Commissioner named and appointed in and by an Act of Parliament made and passed in the Fiftyfifth year of the reign of His present Majesty King George the Third entitled An Act for Inclosing Lands in the Parishes of Rickinghall Superior Rickinghall Inferior and Hinderclay in the County of Suffolk...

...And I the said Commissioner do hereby assign set out and allott unto the Surveyor of the Highways in the Said Parish of Rickinghall Superior for the time being as and for a Public Clay Pit ONE Piece of Land parcel of Micklewood Green containing by measure two roods, bounded by Micklewood Green road North East land allotted to Mary Mann South Land belonging to James Hamblin Smith West and ending in a point North West AND I do hereby direct and appoint that the Said Surveyors shall inclose and fence the said Allotment against the road and against the Allotment to Mary Mann and that they and their Successors Surveyors for the time being of the Said Highways shall forever hereafter maintain and keep in repair the said fences by keeping up the banks and quick and scouring the ditches thereof...

(Suffolk County Council Record Office Folio B150/1/24)

1894 Local Government Act.
The Land was owned by the Parish of Rickinghall Superior.

At the beginning of the 20th Century it was fenced, gated and ditched and was rented out at 6d (2½ p) per annum.

1919 The Land was let to Mr Hugh Bunting for 10/- (50p) per annum.

1935 Poor House Land: 2 years' rent 1/- (5p) per annum.

No more information is available until 1943, when the only item on the agenda for the Parish Council meeting was the letting of Pest House Land for Observation Post. There is anecdotal evidence that a cottage on the site was used as a 'isolation unit, probably for smallpox, leprosy etc. before World War II.

1943 Royal Observer Corps rented the Pest House Land for £1 per annum

1954 The Air Ministry having rented the land from 1943 to 1952 at £1 per annum finally bought it for £2 10s 0d (£2.50).

1956 A further plot of land was bought by the Air Ministry to build an underground monitoring post to complement the tower built during World War II.

The land was given back to Rickinghall Parish Council a few years ago and it was agreed to return the land to a wildlife site.

Chapter 8 The Street from Pound Farm to Fen Lane North Side

Pound Farm is an 18th century building. It was owned by James Hamblin Smith from before 1839 until 1850 when it was put up for sale after his death. At this time it was described as a double tiled cottage occupied by John Talbot and Thomas Gooderham. In 1891 it was again put up for sale on the death of Revd James Coyle. It was occupied at this time by Mr Robinson and was described as a small farmhouse divided into two cottages with a new tiled barn and numerous agricultural buildings. (1) In the 20th century it was farmed by Mr & Mrs Wales. It was sold by them to William Brown of Suggenhall in 1944. Amos (Jo) Brown lived at Number 1 with his family. After they moved out in 1976 it was rented to Barclays Bank, who had a small branch there from 1979 until 1991. His brother Cyril (Billy) lived at Number 2. The barn was converted to a house in the 1980s.

Stone Cottage stands back from The Street. It was a beer house in the late 19th and early 20th century. Bert Matthews lived here. He was a carpenter who made the Tau cross font cover and the altar top for Rickinghall Inferior church.

Village Molecatcher Jim Brown and his wife lived in **Holme Cottage** during the second half of the 20th century. They were no relation to the Browns from Pound Farm or to Basil Brown.

Bothwell House was a bakery owned by Frederick Alford 'Baker and Confectioner' in the early 20th century. (2) In 1936 when it was put up for sale by Miss Coleby it was described as a *'Desirable small freehold business property well situate in The Street, comprising pleasant dwelling-house, shop 15ft x 8ft with show window, counter and shelving, small room used as a tea room; Bake office, fitted with side furnace oven; outbuildings, small yard and garden.'* (3) It obviously did not sell as she finally closed it in the war years. It was bought by Mr Blaker who opened it as a sweet shop. He sold it to Mr & Mrs Teddy Telford, who in turn, sold it to Mr & Mrs Norden, and for many years it was Norden's sweet shop, run by Mrs Norden and her sister Mrs Lawrence.

Basil Brown lived in **Cambria** from the mid 1930s until he died in 1977. He was living there when he discovered the famous ship burial at Sutton Hoo in the summer of 1939. He excavated many sites in the

F Alford, Baker and Confectioner, now Bothwell House

Rickinghall area and also made comprehensive maps of sites of archaeological interest. He had a shed in the back garden in which he kept his finds. This was quite an Aladdin's Cave for the local schoolchildren. He was very good with children and would always spend time explaining anything they wanted to know about the history and archaeology of the area.

The Anchorage is a listed 18th century building.

Jessamine Lodge and **House** is an early 18th century building. It was occupied by the Jolly family in the 18th century. Thomas Jolly, a shopkeeper, left it to his son who in turn left it to the Misses Mary and Susannah Jolly. In 1831 John Algar and James Walker were sentenced at the Bury St Edmunds assizes to be transported to New South Wales for seven years for breaking into the warehouse of Miss Jolly of Rickinghall and stealing 'a quantity of carrots, some sugar and half a firkin of butter'. (4) In 1845 the Misses Jolly sold the premises to William Street who also owned The Golden Lion. He was described as a grocer and draper. (5) A printed bill heading for 'The Royal Chemical Works and Hall of Pharmacy' owned by William Street & Company, suggests he also had a pharmacy on the site. In 1913 Miss Emily Street inherited the house and shop premises from her brother, another William, who had inherited them from their father. She died in 1931. There are photographs of the grocery

The Street, Rickinghall, Suffolk.   1646

Rickinghall Supply Stores in the building now known as Jessamine House

shop in the early 20th century when it was Aldrych & Bryant's shop. In the 1920s it became 'The Rickinghall Supply Stores' run firstly by Mr Baldwin then by Mr Biggs who was also in charge of the Labour Exchange at that time. In the 1930s unemployed people had to report there three times a week to sign on. Doctor Wheatly had his surgery at the other end of the house. After the war it was sold to Mr Hart as a private house, he had the shop front removed and windows matching the others in the house put in. It was divided into two private homes in the late 20th century. A fire insurance plaque on the wall is modern.

Lion House is an 18th century building. The tenement was probably owned by the Houchin family in the 16th century. It passed to Thomas Jolly from John Freeman in 1768. We are told in an affidavit by Gaskin Yeoman dated 1827 that this John Freeman died of smallpox. Gaskin states that he helped at John Freeman's funeral and as a consequence he too caught smallpox. (6) Jolly sold the house to James Smith, a tanner in 1787. (It appears that it was in one large tenement taking in the house and land of Uplands and that of Jessamine House.) In 1848 William Street bought it from Barnard Smith and in 1850 it was reported that he had recently built a brewery next to the house. In 1855 the name 'Golden Lion' is mentioned. He mortgaged the property but was declared bankrupt. The beer house and brewery, including a *steam engine, mill stones, going gears, tackle and machinery, coppers, vats, coolers, mash tub, brewing utensils* were taken over by the creditors. (7) The Golden Lion, cottage and outbuildings were sold to Tollemache's Brewery in 1897. In 1925 Alice Avis ran the pub until about 1945 when Claude Elmer took over. The Golden Lion was a beer house and could not sell spirits. In the

R to L: No 1 Co-op Cottage; The Co-op; Marsden Terrace; Lion Cottage and Lion House

early 1960s the Golden Lion and cottage were sold to Arthur and Ken Bryant. In the mid 20th century Rickinghall bowls club and green were behind the house, where **Lime Tree House** stands today. **Ash House** stands on the site of the brewery.

Marsden Terrace is a row of three 19th Century terraced houses.

The Co-operative Shop was originally situated in the Chilvers building in the Market Place. It moved into a purpose-built shop on The Street in front of the present building in 1929. To the right were two cottages, 1 and 2 Co-op Cottages which were owned by the Co-op, the right hand one of which was for the manager. They were demolished as part of the new development when the 1929 Co-op building was demolished and the Co-op moved to the present site opening in February 2003. Four new houses were then built on the old site.

Uplands is a 17th century house with possible earlier origins. The associated barn is possibly 17th century. The land north of the house appears to have been a tannery for several years. The Enclosure Map of 1819 shows 'Tan yards', north of where the barn stands. In a will of 1810 James Smith left 'the Tanning office, barns & buildings' to Barnard Smith, his son, described as a tanner. (7) The Houchin family had owned this land for many years from the early 17th century. In 1622 Thomas Houchin the elder was described as a tanner. In William Houchin's will of 1652 there was a 'tanning office' in this area. (8) In 2011 the barn was converted into two houses and the mid 20th century bungalow was renovated.

Maypole Meadow was once town lands which were exchanged at the time of the enclosures in 1819. James Hamblin Smith became the new owner.

Walnut-Tree Place is a row of four Victorian terraced brick houses with a date stone showing '1884' on the front. The Enclosure Map of 1819 and an 1850 sales catalogue show two houses on the site. (9) These probably dated from the 17th century. They burnt down before 1884 when the row was built. However number 1 at the end of the row still has much of the original timber framing from the earlier period. In 1850 Thomas Clarke, a cabinet maker, lived in this cottage (described as a 'neat cottage'). In the mid 20th century Mr Davey had his corn and coal business behind these houses.

According to the listing **Hamblyn House** is a 17th century house which was partly rebuilt and extended about 1720. During the 19th century it was the residence of James Hamblin Smith from whom it is thought the house

*L to R : Hamblyn House, Bell Hill House, Edwin Kerry Newsagent,
House now demolished*

derives its name. He attended Botesdale Grammar School and later, like his cousin Barnard Smith Junior, wrote mathematics text books. Barnard Smith's book 'Shilling Arithmetic' provides an interesting insight into the economic life of the mid 19th century. One exercise to be answered was *A labourer earns 12s 6d a week, his wife 4s 9d, and two of his boys 3s 6d each; he has to pay weekly to his club 10½d, and for house rent 1s 6d: what has he left for food and clothing?* The supports holding the porch cover appear to have a scroll and feather quill carved onto them. Could this be a reference to these books? In 1850 after the death of James Hamblin Smith the house and his estate of land were put up for sale. (9) The sales document from this time describes the house as having a *Dining Room, Breakfast Room, Library, Study, Kitchen, Back Kitchen, scullery, Brew-house, Butler's Pantry, Housekeepers room, Dairy and larder on the ground floor with a Drawing Room and small sitting room and six bedrooms, two dressing rooms and a man servants bedroom on the first floor with six attic rooms.* It appears that this was when the Robinson family, who were flour merchants and maltsters, bought the house. They had their malting complex and warehouse here. Early photographs show the warehouse situated between Hamblyn House and Walnut-Tree Place. The Rickinghall Parish School Room had been in this building for a time

R to L: The Bell Inn, two cottages now demolished, Newsagent, Bell Hill House, Hamblyn House, Robinson's warehouse, now demolished and Walnut Tree Terrace.

prior to 1850.

Before 1974 the boundary between East and West Suffolk went through Hamblyn House. The Rickinghall Inferior and Rickinghall Superior boundary still does. In the mid 20th century Harry Goddard had his building yard behind Hamblyn House.

The building that is now **Bell Hill House and The Newsagents** is mid 16th century and was extended in the 17th century. It has a plain crown post roof. The Newsagents was once owned by the Kerry family and we still have one of their account books for the year 1946. At one time a shed was situated across the road opposite the shop to sell the newspapers.

There were once two cottages between the Newsagents and The Bell Inn. In the mid 20th century one was occupied by Mr. Carmen, who was blind and made baskets, the other was Mr Baxter's barbers shop.

The listings for **The Bell Inn** say it dates from the first half of the 17th century. An inn called The Bell was mentioned in a document applying for permission to serve meat during Lent in 1619. In about 1720 it was expanded and the rear wing was added, which was probably when it became a coaching inn. A brewhouse was built at about this time. Pigot's Directory for 1830 says that coaches going between Cambridge and Yarmouth on Tuesdays, Thursdays and Saturdays called here. Coaches to Norwich left on a Monday. At this time James Phillips was the publican. By 1847 Augustus and Miss Belinda Phillips were the licensees. (10) Another James Phillips was the publican in 1884. According to the

1891 and 1901 Censuses the appropriately named Leonard Tipple was the licensed victualler at that time. In 1898 the Deanery Magazine recorded that *The Bell Hotel narrowly escaped being burnt down when a beam in a chimney caught fire but was seen and instantly put out'*. Assembly Rooms were built at the turn of the 19th century and in 1912 Thomas Hupton the proprietor was advertising them.

In the early days of the Second World War Tom Dunkley took over as landlord. Daisy, his wife, was a circus owner in partnership with her sister Rose and her brothers Freddy and Horace Crick. When the war stopped the circus from travelling they moved to The Bell. At that time there was a large row of stables in The Bell yard. It was here and in the field behind that they kept their animals, cats, dogs, geese and a mule. Their miniature horses were kept in the Bell meadows in Fen Lane. They had a parrot in the bar that used to swear at the customers. Tom and Daisy's daughter Olga used to take the performing animals to shows and pantomimes all over England. In 1945 the Bowls Club was re-formed and a green was established behind The Bell. Freddy gave a cup to the Bowls Club, now known as the 'Bell Cup', which is still presented each year. Apparently the actual cup was one Freddy used to present to anyone who could ride his mule in the circus. (11)

Astley House is a 16th century house which was altered and brick faced in the 19th and 20th centuries. For many years prior to 1898 it was part of The Bell. It is said that it was named after a Colonel Astley who ran a troupe of performing horses which he used to overwinter in the fields behind The Bell. He was perhaps a descendant of Philip Astley who had a similar troupe in London in the late 18th century and who invented the circular area for performing. In 1898 the West Suffolk Constabulary leased the building from Lacon & Co, brewers, of Great Yarmouth, who owned both it and The Bell. It was the Rickinghall Police Station until 1968 when it moved to Wattisfield. PC Gosling was the policeman from 1934 until 1953. (12)

Cheyleswood House is a mid to late 17th century house which was extended and altered in the 19th and 20th centuries when a shop window was put in at the east end. In the 1860s Henry Rednall bought two messuages here from the Dobson family who had owned them earlier in the century. He demolished one building which could have been where the old chapel is now situated next to Southgate Farmhouse. It is thought that in 1839 Robert Boston occupied that cottage. He was a tailor and also a hairdresser. In the mid 20th century Miss Hazell had a toy shop in Cheyleswood House, where she also sold sweets.

The building adjoining Southgate Farmhouse was once a Congregational

Chapel, built about 1868, possibly by Henry Rednall on the site of the building he had demolished. For many years until the early 1980s Eric Burroughes had his coach building business here. Recently various other businesses have occupied it. During the Second World War there was a pillbox outside this building. Its guns were aimed towards the Market Place to fire if tanks came that way. The 16th century barn behind the farmhouse was converted into a house in 1985.

Southgate Farmhouse and Beaumont Cottage

Southgate Farmhouse is an early 16th century house which was extended in the 17th and 18th centuries. To the left the parlour cross wing has traces of a shop window, it also has peg holes for shelves. In 1383 Simon Jolyf was fined 12d for 'removing sheep' from the lord of the manor at the time of the 'rumour'. (The name given at the time to what we now call the peasants revolt). (13) He was also fined for not keeping his house in good repair. The entry says that his tenement had a hall house and the land 'stretched' to Adam Skynners house (which was on the corner of Fen Lane and The Street). (14) So it seems from this that he lived where Southgate Farmhouse stands today.

In 1819 Joseph Burroughes owned the tenement. In 1839 it was owned by Mary Burroughes and John Nunn was the tenant farmer. He also had the windmill in Mill Lane. A Robert Southgate was born in 1820 the 11th child of William Southgate who died a year later. Robert was adopted by the Nunn family and was known as Bob Nunn. The story goes that for 30 years from the age of 17 this Robert drove the mail cart from Botesdale to Scole. (15) It was probably his son another Robert Southgate from whom the house name comes. He farmed here in the early part of the 20th century. A report of the Ixworth Petty Sessions in the Diss Express of 18th August 1916 states that he was fined for showing a light in his farmyard at 1 a.m. on 3rd August. Henry Seeley from The Bell and Frank Cook of Botesdale were witnesses saying they had told him to put out the light. He died in 1918 and left the farmhouse to Elizabeth Southgate and her husband Earnest Burroughes, the parents of Eric Burroughes the coachbuilder.

It is possible that the **Market House** is a 17th century house. There is not much timber visible in the house today but it appears that it once had a jetty facing the market. In the 1930s it was a shop, owned by the Misses

Curls, selling haberdashery and sweets. At the outbreak of war they packed up and left. The shop was empty for many years after that.

On the corner of Fen Lane stand three houses; Ash Cottage, Farthings and The Walnuts. These were built in 1973. In the late 14th century Adam Skynner lived on this site. In 1383 he was fined for *'removing 1 pelt at the time of the rumour'*. (16) In 1427 there is reference to a *'tiled house with a tiled kitchen formerly lived in by Adam Skynner'*. (17) A house with a tiled roof, rather than the more common thatched roof, was very unusual in villages at this period. A tile kiln for making bricks and tiles was situated near Botesdale Lodge in the 15th century.

Outside these houses stands a red phone box, which is listed. It originally had the number 1, as it was the first telephone on the Botesdale exchange. Simonds Garage was number 2. (18)

Fen Lane runs from the north side of the Market Place towards what used to be Botesdale Fen. The lane is the boundary between Botesdale and Rickinghall Inferior. The houses on the west side are in Rickinghall Inferior, those on the east are in Botesdale.

(1) Redgrave Estate Papers nos.269 & 396.1 (2) Kelly's Directory 1900 (3) Newspaper article from 1936 (4) Information from Neil Lanham (5) Jessamine House deeds (6) Tipplers house deeds (7) Lion house deeds (8) From research carried out by Graham Clayton (9) Redgrave Estate Papers No:269 (10) 1847 Norfolk Counties Directory (11) Arthur Bryant, P.1 (12) Article by Ken Youngs former owner, History Recorder for Rickinghall 1990s (13) Bacon 27/1 (14) Bacon 27/5 (15) Information from Gilbert Burroughes (16) Bacon 27/2 (17) Bacon 34/13 (18) Jean Sheehan, Parish Magazine December 2004.

View towards Rickinghall Inferior church from the roof of Ridge House

Playing field and Church Meadow from the church tower

Chapter 9 The Street from Garden House Lane to Warren Lane
South side

The Gables and **Gable End** are in one building on the corner of The Street and Garden House Lane. The building is dated to the early to mid 16th century. It was extended in the late 17th century. In 1839 it was owned by Susannah Smith. Jonathan Blowers rented part of it from her. He and his son, also Jonathan, were cabinet and chair manufacturers, making the famous 'Mendlesham' chairs. They had their business here in the 1830s and 1840s. (1) In 1970 it was proposed that the building be demolished but after a public enquiry it was reprieved. (2) The Gables was the first house in Suffolk to be restored by the Suffolk Buildings Preservation Trust. This was in 1973. The initials S H in metal on the east end of The Gables were said by Basil Brown to stand for Stephen Howchin. The date 1748 is engraved on the letter H. However no reference has yet been found to a Stephen Howchin living at this time.

There used to be three cottages between Gable End and Garden House Lane, however they were demolished in the mid 1930s. In 1839 they were occupied by George Fordham 'and others'. In 1880 they were for sale and one was at that time in the occupation of James Fordham. They were sold to Charles Silver together with Willow Cottage for £105.

Elm Cottage was built in the late 15th century perhaps as early as 1475. Inside there is a medieval shop window dating from the 15th or early 16th century. The cottage was faced with brick in the 19th century. Thomas Talbot is the earliest occupant so far traced. He married in Rickinghall Superior church in 1566. After he died in 1589 an inventory of his goods mentioned *"one blind hores And one moar 30s"* (one blind horse and one more

Audrey and June Banham outside their parent's sweet shop

30s). His wife Joanna was the owner of the house in 1608. William Wiffen, a baker, lived here from 1634. In an inventory taken when he died in 1662 there is reference to a 'one horse mill' in the grounds, presumably this was to grind his corn. After he died the Stanton family occupied the cottage until 1721 when Nathaniel Freeman took over the copyhold. The Freeman family held the cottage until 1760 when Samuel Goldsmith, who had married Sarah Freeman, sold it to James Debenham.

Between 1841 and 1912 the cottage was home to a family of wheelwrights called Bullock and the garden contained a number of large sheds. The first of this family was Henry, the illegitimate son of Ann Bullock of Wortham. He started a thriving business and lived into his eighties. He married Eliza Blowers, daughter of Jonathan Blowers the chair maker. In 1922 Emma Banham bought the cottage and she and her husband Harry lived there for about 40 years. For many years they had a sweet shop in the front room. (3)

15th C shop window in Elm Cottage

There appears to have been a row of about four small cottages and shops between Elm Cottage and The Pump House (where Woodnook Cottage and Pavilion House stand today). They were set back from the road, level with The Pump House, with gardens in front of them.

Woodnook Cottage is a bungalow that was built in 1948/9 for Mr Carlton, the manager of Aldrich & Bryant's the grocers shop next door.

Pavilion House was built fronting the road in the early 20th century. It was Aldrich & Bryant's grocers shop in the early 20th century and remained Mr Warner's grocers shop until the late 1980s, when it became a private house.

The Pump House is an early 16th century house which was probably owned by the Howchin family in the 16th and 17th centuries. A series of photographs taken by Edmund Farrer from March to July 1926 recorded the medieval house being repaired and a garage being built in front of it. As well as selling petrol, the garage also carried out motor repairs, hired out lorries and also had a taxi service. The lane between the Pump House and Prospect House led to the yard where Mr Perry, the owner kept his lorries. After the garage closed in the 1980s there was an antiques shop in the Pump House for many years.

Prospect House was the home of the Moule family from 1918 when James and Rebecca moved here from Hopton. Two of their sons, Gordon and Victor, were killed in the First World War. Their names are on the Hopton War Memorial. Another son, Herman who was a 'ladder maker' and decorator, lived here until 1960. In front of the house facing The Street was a small shop called at one time 'The Central Stores'. In the 1930s it was a fish shop run by Mr Philips, whose wife taught at the school. After that it was a greengrocers run for a short time from 1953 by Mr & Mrs Brier, then by the Myhill family and then for many years by Mr Chew. It closed in the 1970s. At this time the house and shop were owned by Mr Perry and his sons who also owned the Pump House and the garage. The house behind Prospect House was lived in by Mr Perry's

April 1926. Fish shop in Prospect House, Pump House being renovated

sisters and was demolished when the Ryders Way development took place.

Pump house repaired and garage in operation July 1926

The deeds of **Kent House** date to 1761 when a John Smith, the copyhold tenant, died and left to his son, also John, the *'premises the said John Smith the Father had took up to him at a Court held 11 Oct 1711 on the surrender of Sarah Green'*. (4) From this it appears the house was built before 1711. In 1794 William Candler a cooper became the tenant. In 1929 Mr & Mrs Chilvers bought the premises and opened their drapery shop here before moving to the market site in 1935. Mr Biggs' son moved his newsagents from across the road in Jessamine House and in the 1940s he sold the business to Mr Kerry at 'The Newsagents'. The house was later sold to Bill Edrich the cricketer who played for Middlesex and England and was the father of John Edrich, who also played for England.

Raleigh House is an 18th century listed building which was altered in the 19th century. In the 18th century John Chandler was the tenant. At one time it is understood to have been a 'flop' house, where very cheap accommodation could be had. There were probably mattresses in the attic but it is said that if all these were taken ropes were slung across on which people could lean! The Hales family have lived here since 1954.

Two thatched cottages between Cloister Cottage and Ridge House were demolished in 1919. A photograph from earlier in the 20th century shows

The Street Rickinghall
L: Cloister Cottage, Rayleigh House, Kent House, Prospect House
R: Co-op, Marsden Terrace, Lion Cottage, Lion House

them in a very poor state with the windows boarded up. In 1919 before they were demolished they were described as being in a 'ruined' condition.

Ridge House was built in the 18th century and was known as Spring View until the 1940s when the name was changed to Ridge House. It was extended to the front and 'gentrified' in the 19th century. In the late 19th century William Rush a veterinary surgeon lived here. The barn, old stable and coach house were probably built at the time of the original small house which appears to have belonged to The Homestead for many years. The coach house and stable were still being used for their original purpose in the late 1930s, with the coachman living above the coach house. According to Basil Brown a Roman burial was discovered in the garden in the 1920s by William Foulgar who was employed by the owner Mr Lanman. A grey ware vessel known as a 'folded beaker' discovered at the same time is now in the Ipswich Museum. (5) Two steel girders were inserted into the cellar ceiling during the Second World War so it could be used as an air raid shelter. They are still in place.

Between Ridge House and The Homestead, where the drive now runs, there was once a lane called Browns Lane. This was closed in 1819.

The Homestead is a mid to late 17th century house. The deeds go back to 1733 when John Elmy left his lands to his brother George. This family owned a great deal of land in both Rickinghall and Botesdale in the early to mid 18th century. Richard Todd, a stonemason, took up the tenancy in the late 1780s. He owned all the land and properties from the present Post Office, Hillside, to The Homestead. In 1823 he sold it to Robert Sword then described as a carpenter. The land stretching from behind The Homestead to Garden House Lane went with the house and was called Home Field. Robert Sword's nephew Benjamin Taylor inherited the property in 1843 and Benjamin's son Charles sold it to Peter Larsen in 1878. Mrs Larsen's nephew G L Gumprecht inherited it and owned the house until 1901. It was called St George's House in the late 19th century and was changed to The Homestead in the early 20th century. In 1935 Dr Ward bought the property. He later had his house and surgery here. Dr Ryder Richardson purchased it after the war. It was the doctor's surgery for the villages until The Health Centre was built in 1982. (6)

There were four cottages situated between The Homestead and Botesdale Post Office, two of which were thatched and two had slate roofs. These burnt down in 1935. According to a newspaper article the fire was started by fireworks which had been let off in the garden that evening. (7) The Goddard family, Mr & Mrs Boyce, Mrs Plume and Mr & Mrs John Ray were the families left homeless by the fire. The site of the two nearest to The Homestead was purchased by Dr Ward in 1939. He used the site to build an extension to house his surgery. **Northdene** was built on the site of the other two cottages.

Botesdale Post Office, previously known as **Hillside**, is actually in Rickinghall Superior. The Post Office has been here since the late 1940s. When the earlier Post Office in the Market Place closed no suitable building could be found in Botesdale in which to house it. This is why although in Rickinghall it is called Botesdale Post Office. The house was built in the mid 1700s. In his will dated 1766 Thomas Randall Senior, a blacksmith, left his house furniture and *'broad wheele wagon'* to his wife; to Peter his son he left *'all his working tools & stock in trade'*. Until 1826 the house was owned by Richard Todd. (8) He was the stonemason who rebuilt the tower of Redgrave church in 1784. It was built with 'Woolpit' white bricks probably to complement Redgrave Hall which was built of the same bricks. 'Todd built me in 1784' is inscribed on the top of the church tower. (9) In the 19th century Elizabeth Garland owned all the houses from Warren Lane to The Homestead including the four cottages which later burned down.

The Post Box is unusual as the main box is from the time of George V, but it has an Edward VII door. This was cobbled together when a bigger one

PART OF STREET, RICKINGHALL.

L: Warren's butchers shop with Hillside
and , in the background, the four cottages which burnt down
R: Robinson's warehouse; Walnut-Tree Terrace

was needed by the late 1990's and was installed in 2000.

Walnut Tree House is a timber-framed house the front part of which is possibly late 17th century or early 18th century, an extension was put on at the back a little later. 'Faiths' shop was a butcher's shop in the 19th and early 20th centuries. The abattoir was in a building on the site of Dunkley's motor services garage. A post with a ring in it for tethering animals was found there. In 1839 Richard Wiseman, a butcher, was the tenant occupying the building. In the Norfolk Counties Directory for 1847 it was advertised as being run by Mrs Susan Wiseman. In 1866 William Warren, a butcher, bought the building from Elizabeth Garland. His son Stephen took over the business from him and was still running it in 1933. In the First World War William Warren, Stephen's eldest son, who had emigrated to Canada, came back to fight. He was killed in 1916 at the age of 28. Stephen's other son Noel took over the business and it was a butchers shop until he retired in the 1960s.

Walnut Tree House is situated next to **Warren Lane**. The lane is the boundary between Rickinghall and Botesdale. It continues along the footpath which leads to and across the bypass. This was called the Procession Way in the medieval period until at least the 18th century. In medieval times, at Rogationtide, there would have been a procession,

66

with hand bells, banners, the parish cross and loud singing, going around the boundary of the whole village. This was called 'beating the bounds' and was to make sure the young people knew the village boundaries, but more importantly it was also to drive the evil spirits from the village. If a procession met one from the neighbouring village there would often be a fight as each thought the demons were being driven over the boundary into their village. (10) The Rickinghall Inferior Churchwardens' account books for the early years of the 19th century record that 'Beating the bounds' still continued in 1800 and 1814.

A mill is shown on the 1819 Enclosure Map, and also on a map from 1850, not far from where Bunny Hollow stands today. So far no information has been found about this mill. In the later 19th and early 20th century there was a mill standing further to the east overlooking Bridewell Lane.

(1) Cotton, Bernard, Pp. 241-245 (2) EAD 21st April 1970 (3) Research by Graham Clayton (4) Kent House deeds (5) Basil Brown's notebooks (6) The Homestead deeds (7) Diss Express 1.7.2005 (8) Hillside deeds (9) Redgrave Church Guidebook by Jean Sheehan (10) Duffy P.136

We at Quatrefoil hope you have enjoyed this walk and found the book a useful guide to the houses of Rickinghall and their histories. To help you explore the neighbouring village of Botesdale a companion guide has been written called 'A Walk Through Botesdale'.

Bibliography: Original Sources

Extents: An extent or survey is a written description of a manor, of the people who rented the land, what they paid and of what services they owed to the lord of the manor. Unfortunately before the 17th century they were very rarely accompanied by maps. The following are the extents used in this work

1289 Extent Redgrave, Add 14850, London, British Library

1437 Extent Rickinghall, Add 14850, London, British Library.

1543 Extent Rickinghall, Add 40063, London, British Library.

1608 Extent Rickinghall, HA 240/2508/1466, SROI.

1641 Extent Rickinghall, HA 240/2508/1472, SROI.

1849 Survey of Redgrave Estate, Redgrave papers

The 'Bacon Collection' was bought from the Redgrave Estate by the University of Chicago in the 1920s. They catalogued and gave the documents manuscript numbers which are the numbers used here. i.e. Bacon Ms 21 Court Rolls = B21 CR http://www.lib.uchicago.edu/e/spcl/findaid/bacon/all.html last accessed 23.7.2013

Directories: These are trade directories which were published in various years by various publishers, the main ones being Kelly's, White's and the Post Office Directories.

Enclosure Map and Schedules: These were published when the common lands were enclosed in the early 19th century. In Rickinghall Inferior and Superior this was in 1819. Enclosure Map and Schedule SROI B150/1/2.4. Any 1819 date in the text means it is from this.

Tithe Map: These surveys were produced throughout the country to record the tithes owed to the Church. In Rickinghall Inferior and Superior this was done in 1839. Tithe Map and Apportionment SROI F122/C2/3a. Any 1839 date in the text means it is from this.

Edmund Farrer's papers SROI HD 78/2671 Rickinghall. These are papers collected by Revd Edmund Farrer. There are also files for Redgrave and Botesdale.

Bibliography: Books and Articles

A Millennium Miscellany, The Heritage Circle (2000).

Brown, Basil, *Suffolk Explorations*, unpublished

Brown, Basil, *Notebooks*, unpublished

Bryant, Arthur, '*Bowls in Botesdale and Rickinghall*' (2005)

Buck, Sarah, *Memories of William & Sarah Buck* aged 91 years (1997)

Copinger, W.A, *The Manors of Suffolk Notes on Their History and Devolution*, T. Fisher Unwin (London, 1905) Vol.I and Vol.III

Cotton, Bernard (Dr), *The English Regional Chair* published by Antiques Collectors Club, Woodbridge [ISBN 1 85149 023x]

Duffy, Eamon, *The Stripping of the Altars Traditional Religion in England c.1400-c.1580*, Yale University Press (New Haven and London, 1992)

Flowerdew, A. Knox, *Rickinghall in the County of Suffolk*

Mee, Arthur, *The King's England Suffolk* Hodder and Stoughton (London 1941)

Northeast, Peter, Transcription of Wills from the Register 'Gelour' NRO unpublished

Rackham, Oliver, *The History of the Countryside*, Phoenix (London 1997)

English Heritage Grade II Listings – www.ImagesofEngland last accessed 27.7.2013

Glossary

Abuttal	Land abutting on to the north, south, east and west boundaries of a piece of land being described in an extent
Camping or Camp Ball	A game something like football dating from the medieval period
Carpenters' marks	Roman numerals scribed onto timbers to help with the assembly of the building
Chancery Records	Chancery Court handled civil disputes for England and Wales. The Records are now held in the PRO
Chantry	Endowment for priests to sing masses for founder's soul. Chapel, so endowed
Chive chamber	Where the chives or dried rootlets from the barley grain (also called malt culms) were stored
Court books	Business of the 17th – 19th century manor court written into books rather than on to rolls of parchment
Court rolls	Business of the medieval manor court written on to rolls of parchment, usually in Latin
Crown post	Supporting framework or structure of a medieval roof
Demesne	Land within a manor allocated to the lord for his own use
Dragon post	External support of the diagonal inner dragon beam in a building that has a jetty on two adjacent sides
Extent	See 'Original Sources'
Feet of Fines	Records of civil cases heard in the Court of Common Pleas. These are now held in the PRO
Field walking	Systematic walking of an area to check for evidence of archaeological interest
Firkin	Small cask for liquid, butter etc.
Hundred	Subdivision of a county

Lobby entrance house	Front door leads into a small lobby against the side of the chimney
Manor court	In the medieval period this dealt with civil litigation, land transactions, damage and trespass against the lord's property. In later years it usually dealt with land transactions
Messuage	Plot of land containing a dwelling house and outbuildings
Mills	
Post	This has a box shaped body mounted and turning on a vertical main shaft. This is the earliest type of windmill dating from the 12th century
Smock	Developed in the 17th century it is an octagonal shaped mill with sloping, boarded sides which resemble a countryman's smock
Tower	Made of stone, brick or masonry and is cylindrical in shape
Open hall house	Houses with the main room or hall open to the roof, heated by a central hearth
Parvise	Room over the porch of a church for the use of the priest or for storage
Pightle	An enclosed yard or croft, often adjoining a dwelling house
Stipend	Salary
Storey post	A main vertical timber supporting load-bearing horizontal timbers
Tenement	A landholding
Town Land	Land owned by the village

People mentioned in the text:

The **Revd Edmund Farrer** (1848-1935) was Curate of Rickinghall Inferior then Rector of Hinderclay and a historian who wrote articles for the journal East Anglian Miscellany.

Basil Brown was the local archaeologist from Rickinghall, who excavated the ship burial at Sutton Hoo in 1939. He carried out many excavations in the Rickinghall and Botesdale area.

Pre decimal Currency

1 shilling (12d) = 5p

2 shillings and 6 pence (2/6d) = 12 ½ p

5 shillings = 25p

20 shillings = £1

Measurements

1 rod, pole or perch = 16 feet 6 inches

1 foot (12 inches) = 30 cm

40 perches = 1 rood

4 roods = 1 acre

1 acre = 0.4 hectare